CAMBRIDGE PAPERS IN SOCIAL ANTHROPOLOGY

No. 1

D1244569

THE DEVELOPMENTAL CYCLE
IN DOMESTIC GROUPS

THE DEVELOPMENTAL CYCLE
IN DOMESTIC GROUPS

EDITED BY

JACK GOODY

CAMBRIDGE

AT THE UNIVERSITY PRESS

1971

PUBLISHED BY
THE SYNDICS OF THE CAMBRIDGE UNIVERSITY PRESS

Bentley House, 200 Euston Road, London NW1 2DB
American Branch: 32 East 57th Street, New York, N.Y.10022

© CAMBRIDGE UNIVERSITY PRESS 1958

Library of Congress Catalogue Card Number: 78-160087

Standard Book Numbers:
0 521 05116 9 clothbound
0 521 09660 X paperback

First printed 1958
Reprinted 1962
1965
1969
1971

First printed in Great Britain at the University Press, Cambridge
Reprinted in Great Britain by Willmer Brothers Limited, Birkenhead

CONTENTS

CONTRIBUTORS TO THIS ISSUE

MEYER FORTES, William Wyse Professor of Social Anthropology in the University of Cambridge, author of *The Dynamics of Clanship among the Tallensi* (1945), *The Web of Kinship among the Tallensi* (1949), *Kinship and the Social Order* (1970); editor, *African Political Systems* (1940), *Social Structure, Essays Presented to A. R. Radcliffe-Brown* (1949).

J. D. FREEMAN, completed his Ph.D. at Cambridge in 1953 after having done fieldwork in Samoa and Sarawak; at present Reader in Social Anthropology in the Australian National University; author of *Iban Agriculture* (1955).

JACK GOODY has worked among the LoDagaa and the Gonja of the Northern Territories of Ghana and is now Lecturer in Social Anthropology and Director of the African Studies Centre in the University of Cambridge; author of *The Social Organization of the LoWiili* (1956), *Death, Property and the Ancestors* (1962), *Comparative Studies in Kinship* (1969), *Technology, Tradition and the State* (1970), *The Bagre Myth* (1970); editor, *Literacy in Traditional Societies* (1968).

DERRICK J. STENNING, took his Ph.D. in Cambridge in 1954 and later became Director of the Institute of Social and Economic Research, Makerere, Uganda, until his death in 1964. Author of *Savannah Nomads* (1959).

E. R. LEACH, Provost of King's College and Reader in Social Anthropology in the University of Cambridge, has carried out research in Burma, Ceylon, Sarawak and Kurdistan. Numerous publications include *Political Systems of Highland Burma* (1954) and *Pul Eliya, a Village in Ceylon* (1961).

PREFACE

This is the first of a series of occasional papers in social anthropology published by the Cambridge University Press for the Department of Archaeology and Anthropology of the University of Cambridge. We plan to publish further volumes at intervals of about a year. Each volume will be edited by one member of the editorial board and will contain a number of papers arising out of the anthropological research work carried out in the Department. Each volume will deal, as far as possible, with a single, broad topic of theoretical interest. In accordance with the practice that is now well established in social anthropology, the main contributions will take the form of papers based on field research in particular areas and communities. In addition, we intend to include in each volume an introductory paper in which the main theoretical issues referred to in the other papers will be explicitly discussed.

It must be made clear that we are not aiming to produce a series of comprehensive comparative studies. We are primarily interested in developing better concepts, stricter methods of examining field data, and hypotheses suitable for testing in field research. For this purpose, we shall make use of cross-cultural data of limited range, examined in depth. Moreover, the analysis of this data will have been presented and discussed at seminars in which the editors and most of the contributors have participated. It is our belief that this procedure has much to offer for the development of theory in social anthropology.

This, the first number of the series, has arisen out of work upon which Professor Meyer Fortes and some of his students at Cambridge have been engaged over the past few years. It has been edited by Dr J. R. Goody, and Professor Fortes has contributed an introductory paper. Thanks are due to the Behavioural Sciences Division of the Ford Foundation for a personal research grant to Professor Fortes which provided research assistance for the present publication.

The second number of the series will use materials from India, Ceylon and Pakistan to help clarify certain aspects of the concept of caste. It will be edited by E. R. Leach, who will also contribute the general introduction.

We are indebted to the Smuts Memorial Fund of the University of Cambridge for a grant in aid of the publication of this series.

MEYER FORTES
JACK GOODY
E. R. LEACH

INTRODUCTION

By MEYER FORTES

The papers in the present symposium stem from field research and seminar discussions that have been in progress at Cambridge for four or five years. The most promising advance in recent research on the social structures of homogeneous societies has been the endeavour to isolate and conceptualize the time factor. By this I do not mean the amorphous subject matter usually labelled 'culture change' or 'social change'. I mean the more fundamental and difficult problems involved in the truism that the idea of society, the notion of a social system or a social structure, necessarily implies extension through a stretch of time. A social system, by definition, has a life. It is a social system, that particular social system, only so long as its elements and components are maintained and adequately replaced; and the replacement process is the crucial one because the human organism has a limited life span. Maintenance and replacement are temporal phenomena. It is the processes by which they are ensured that concern us when we study the time factor in social structure.

These processes have biological determinants. One is the life span of the individual; the other is the physical replacement of every generation by the next in the succession of death and birth. We must leave to physiology, genetics and demography the exact study of these determinants. It is enough to remind ourselves that a social system will not persist if the average life span of its members is too short for them to have offspring and to rear them to the age when they in turn can have offspring, or, in demographic terms, if the balance of births and deaths does not yield a net reproduction rate of unity or more. From the anthropological point of view, the important thing is that the physical growth and development of the individual is embodied in the social system through his education in the culture of his society, and the succession of the generations through their incorporation in the social structure. The facts of physical continuity and replacement are thus converted into the process of social reproduction.

These generalities can be put in another way. For a social system to maintain itself its two vital resources must be maintained at an adequate level by continuous use and replacement. These two resources are its human capital and its social capital, and it is the latter that specially concerns the anthropologist. It consists of the total body of knowledge and skills, values and beliefs, laws and morals, embodied in the customs and institutions of a society and of the utilities made available for supporting the livelihood of its members through the application of the cultural outfit to natural resources. The process of social reproduction, in broad terms, includes all those institutional mechanisms and customary activities and norms which serve to maintain, replenish and transmit the social capital from generation to generation; and it is with various aspects of this process that all the papers in our symposium are concerned.

Of course generalizations of this sort are not susceptible of investigation by observation and experiment, nor do they lend themselves to profitable theoretical discussion. They are useful only as a step in the task of giving empirical content to the study of the time factor in social structure. They lead us to ask what are the institutional mechanisms and customary activities of social reproduction in a particular society and how do they operate? The nodal mechanism is well known. In all human societies, the workshop, so to speak, of social reproduction, is the domestic group. It is this group which must remain in operation over a stretch of time long enough to rear offspring to the stage of physical and social reproductivity if a society is to maintain itself. This is a cyclical process. The domestic group goes through a cycle of development analogous to the growth cycle of a living organism. The group as a unit retains the same form, but its members, and the activities which unite them, go through a regular sequence of changes during the cycle which culminates in the dissolution of the original unit and its replacement by one or more units of the same kind.

I shall later explain why it is useful to distinguish between the *domestic group* and the *family*, in the strict sense. Here I am interested in a different distinction. It is now commonly agreed that it is necessary, for analytical purposes, to distinguish between the domestic field of social relations, institutions and activities, viewed from within as an internal system, and the politico-jural field, regarded as an external system. A significant feature of the developmental cycle of the domestic group is that it is at one and the same time a process within the internal field and a movement governed by its relations to the external field.

To investigate this process in a given society we must first establish what the domestic group is in that society. The conventional ethnographic method is to give a generalized description derived from the observation of casually selected examples and couched in terms of stereotyped persons and institutions. This is like the amateur demography of travellers and colonial officials in the days before rigorous census methods were introduced. To find out what the average family size was in a primitive community, one rounded up twenty or thirty women at random and questioned them about their children. One then divided the total number of living children recorded by the total number of women and so obtained an 'average'. Such data are now regarded as useless, owing partly to the faulty sampling method, but chiefly to the failure to take into account age differences among the women questioned. Similarly, if we wish to determine reliably the structure and boundaries of the domestic group in a given society, it is essential to use a reliable and representative sample of domestic groups, and more particularly, to take into account their 'age-specific' characters—that is, the stages of the developmental cycle. A domestic group comprising only two successive generations is at a different stage from one made up of three generations; and so is one in which all the filial generation are pre-adolescent as compared with one with some or all the children at marriageable ages. The developmental factor is intrinsic to domestic organization and to ignore it leads to serious misinterpretation of the descriptive facts. The papers here presented demonstrate this, perhaps the most vivid example being that of the Fulani.

Residence patterns illustrate this very well. We know that they provide a basic index of the boundaries of the internal structure of domestic groups. But they are not a primary factor of social structure of the order of kinship, descent, marriage and citizenship. The alignments of residence are determined by the economic, affective, and jural relations that spring from these primary factors, and it is fallacious to analyse them in terms of ostensibly discrete rules or types that come into effect at marriage. There are numerous examples in the descriptive literature of kinship, but a timely and particularly pertinent one is a recent paper by Goodenough.

There are, as he notes, several distinct questions involved. First, there is the question of the normal residential composition of the domestic group in the society. He shows how two investigators can arrive at totally discrepant conclusions about the incidence of different 'types' of residence in the same community though they use what seem to be the same census methods. In fact the source of the apparent discrepancies is the neglect by both investigators of the developmental dimension. Dr Stenning, Dr Freeman and Dr Goody could easily have classified the domestic groups they encountered by types. In each of these communities we can, if we wish, find several 'types'—a 'nuclear family' type, an 'extended patrilocal (virilocal?)' type, an 'extended matrilocal (uxorilocal?)' type, and so forth, with, perhaps, a class of mixed types to eke out the classification. But when it is recognized that these so-called types are in fact phases in the developmental cycle of a single general form for each society, the confusion vanishes. Residence patterns are the crystallization, at a given time, of the development process.

Secondly, there is quite a different problem when we consider residential alignments from the point of view of the person rather than from that of the domestic group as a unit. Genetical analysis then needs to be supplemented by the numerical and conceptual isolation of the structural and cultural variables involved. Marriage is certainly a crucial element in determining

3

choice of residence by or for a person. In developmental terms, the reason for this is because marriage leads to an actual or incipient split in one or both of the spouses' natal families and domestic groups, and fission in the domestic group is always translated into spatial representation in the residence arrangements. In analytical terms, this developmental moment is the starting point of a redistribution of control over productive and reproductive resources associated with a change in the jural status of the spouses. Other things being equal, a wife will reside with her husband if he, or whoever has jural authority over him, has unrestricted rights over her sexual and economic services and her reproductive powers, and children will reside with those who have similar powers over, and the concomitant responsibilities towards, them. Only numerical analysis can show what 'degree of freedom', if any, exists.

A comparison of the Iban situation with that of the Fulani or LoDagaba shows this very clearly. A Fulani wife has no choice. Before she becomes a mother she is under her father's jural authority and resides in his camp; when she becomes a mother she comes wholly under her husband's authority and consequently moves to reside permanently with him. Among the Iban there is ostensibly more choice. One could say that post-marital residence is either virilocal or uxorilocal at will. What in fact happens is that marriage precipitates fission, and its concomitant economic partition, in the natal domestic group of one of the spouses, and this spouse moves out of the group. Which of the spouses moves depends on the stage in the developmental cycle reached by the domestic group at the time of the marriage. If the domestic group consists of parents and two or more children and the one who marries is the oldest of the siblings, he or she will normally move out irrespective of sex. But if the marrying one is the last child remaining in the family after the others have married and hived off, he or she stays on as prospective heir to the parents and is joined in his or her natal home by the spouse. Whether a married couple reside 'virilocally' or 'uxorilocally' is, therefore, not an arbitrary choice but depends upon which of them is seceding from his or her natal *bilek*. This is correlated with the developmental stage of the *bilek*, but to see why this is so we must understand the forces behind *bilek* fission. What they come down to is the jural principles and economic requirements which give the conjugal bond precedence over the sibling bond in the social structure and vest authority and power over productive and reproductive resources in the married partners.

We can set up a paradigm distinguishing three main stages or phases in the developmental cycle of the domestic group. First there is a phase of expansion that lasts from the marriage of two people until the completion of their family of procreation. The biological limiting factor here is the duration of the wife's (or wives') fertility. In structural terms it corresponds to the period during which all the offspring of the parents are economically, affectively and jurally

4

dependent on them. Secondly, and often overlapping the first phase in time (hence my preference for the term 'phase' instead of 'stage'), there is the phase of dispersion or fission. This begins with the marriage of the oldest child and continues until all the children are married. Where the custom by which the youngest child remains to take over the family estate is found, this commonly marks the beginning of the final phase. This is the phase of replacement, which ends with the death of the parents and the replacement in the social structure of the family they founded by the families of their children, more specifically, by the family of the father's heir amongst the children. Turning again to the Iban, we can see that if the oldest and youngest children of a *bilek* are both male, then the former's marriage marks the onset of the phase of dispersion and he will reside 'uxorically', whereas the marriage of the latter marks the end of the cycle and his wife will reside 'virilocally'. But these superficially contrary choices are really alternative 'phase-specific' expressions of the same set of structural factors.

Mutatis mutandis this paradigm can be applied to all social systems. The birth of a couple's first child, so frequently picked out by special ritual observances, which initiates the phase of expansion, and the marriage of their oldest child, which precipitates the eventual dissolution and replacement of their domestic group, are always critical episodes in the developmental cycle. But they are not, of course, the only critical turning points. The initiation, retirement, or death of a member of the group may be equally important.

In short, by the structural and cultural variables involved in the developmental cycle I mean all the forces generated by the social structure, and all the customs and institutions through which these forces and the values they reflect are manifested. Biological laws ensure that children inexorably grow up if they are not cut off by death. Growing up requires a minimum time span, at least fifteen years for the attainment of physiological maturity, and often rather longer for the attainment of social maturity. The complex and fundamental tasks of child-rearing imposed on the domestic group by this fact generates critical forces for its cycle of development.

The most important of these forces is the opposition between successive generations focused in the incest taboos. This is not a static condition. The opposition develops in intensity and may change in its customary forms of expression during the time that the filial generation is growing up. It is a factor in the partial or complete secession of offspring at marriage; for the essential stake is the right to use and dispose of the productive and reproductive resources which every generation must gain possession of when it reaches maturity. This is documented in all the papers of our symposium. Its theoretical implications are cogently stated by Dr Goody, and confirmed in Dr Stenning's analysis. Among the Fulani we see very clearly how growing up, for a boy, is projected into the social structure through his increasing skill and responsibility in cattle husbandry and the corresponding extension of his rights in herd ownership, and culminates, after his marriage and achievement of fatherhood, in the dispossession and virtual expulsion of his father from the productive and reproductive organization of the domestic group. In general, the allocation by gift, prestation, inheritance and succession of rights over property, persons and office on the one hand, and of rights over the fertility of women on the other, is a major, if not the most significant, factor in the developmental cycle of the domestic group.

Now the opposition between successive generations operates primarily within the internal structure of the domestic group. But it is legitimized and kept within bounds through being allowed customary expression in forms sanctioned by the total society. Marriage, inheritance, succession, and so forth, are events in the internal system, or, to be more specific, domain of the domestic group; but they are simultaneously events in the external domain, where the domestic group is integrated into the total social structure in its political, jural and ritual aspects. The interests involved are those of society at large as well as those of the domestic group *per se*. This is shown in many customary forms, e.g. in the conjunction of rules of exogamy with rules of incest in the regulation of marriage, in the obligatory participation of extra-domestic kin and of political authorities in funeral ceremonies and in decisions about inheritance and succession, in initiation ceremonies, and so on. That is to say, it is through political, jural and ritual institutions and customs which derive their force from society at large that the interests of the total social system, as opposed to those specific to the domestic domain, are brought to bear on the latter. Classificatory kinship institutions, unilineal descent corporations, age sets, and the great variety of institutions and organizations through the medium of which citizenship is exercised, are the structural links between the two domains. We now have a number of excellent studies showing how the domestic group and the unilineal descent group are interlocked. The former is the source from which the latter is continually replenished. This is not just a matter of physical recruitment. There is a 'feeding in' process by which the differentiation of persons in the domestic domain by generation, filiation, and descent, is projected into the structure of the unilineal descent group to generate the modes of collocation and segmentation so characteristic of lineage systems. It is a continuous process that goes on as long as a lineage endures.

But there is a feature of this process that can easily be overlooked. It is true that fission in the domestic group can be regarded as the model and starting point of segmentation in the lineage, if we are concerned with the internal growing points of the lineage as a temporal system. But if we look at lineage systems from the point of view of their place in the external politico-jural domain and consider their connection with the domestic domain from that angle, we can see that differentiation and fission in the domestic group are reciprocally determined by norms and rules derived from the external domain. The classical example is descent rules.

Dr Goody's paper shows very neatly what I have in mind. He has an ideal comparative situation among the LoDagaba and the LoWiili. These two communities have the same farming system and the same pattern of household economy. Their jural and ritual concepts and values are the same. The only significant difference in social structure between the two communities lies in their descent rules. In one, rights over productive and reproductive resources are held and transmitted in accordance with patrilineal norms, in the other most of them are subject to matrilineal norms. What he shows is that this alternative creates differences in the mode and direction of fission in the domestic group, the critical factor being the rules of inheritance and succession by which property rights are allocated between successive generations. By contrast, among the Iban, who do not have unilineal descent concepts, it is the primacy of the marriage bond over the bonds of filiation and siblingship that gives direction to the process of *bilek* fission and its material accompaniment, the partition of the *bilek* estate.

Classificatory kinship systems are not coterminous with unilineal descent systems, as the Iban material shows. When we consider how they serve to link the domestic domain with the politico-jural domain, new problems arise. That is why Dr Leach's application of the developmental frame of analysis in his reinterpretation of the Trobriand kinship system is of special interest. The point to seize on, it seems to me, is the connection he postulates between kinship nomenclature, shifts in residence alignments, and changes in the jural status of men and women through the life cycle. This resolves many of the obscurities in Malinowski's accounts of Trobriand kinship customs and institutions.

Dr Leach's analysis holds for other societies in which matrilineal descent is followed. By this rule of descent, a boy has one jural status as his father's son and a different one as his mother's brother's nephew. The latter status is distinguished by the fact that it alone confers rights of inheritance and succession to property, office and ritual authority. In the Trobriands, a boy lives with his parents in his natal family and domestic group during his jural infancy. This lasts until he is deemed to be of an age when he is fit to assume the claims and rights to which he is entitled by matrilineal descent. These include rights of inheritance and succession and the consequential rights of citizenship in his clan community. This change of jural status is legitimized by his moving out to reside with his mother's brother. He cannot, of course, enter into possession of his hereditary estate until his uncle dies; but his claims on it are thus staked for society to see and approve. Thus a boy's formative years are passed under his father's care and it is from his father that he receives the training in the skills, beliefs and values of his society. Then, when he is ready to take a responsible place in society, he moves, physically as well as jurally, into the social orbit where his adult status is effective. For a girl there is a similar shift in status and residence when she leaves her childhood home with her parents, where she has been a daughter and a sister, to join her husband as his wife and the future mother of his children. Since a woman is bound to live with her husband after marriage, she cannot share a brother's residence, for she may not, by the rules of clan exogamy, marry a clansman. Opposite sex sibling avoidance rules fit into this arrangement, and as the local community may be segmented into clan localities, a woman cannot, after marriage, live in the same locality as her brother even though it is her own clan area. The developmental cycle of the domestic group is thus tied into the local and clan organization through a division of functions related to the transition from jural infancy to jural adulthood of the filial generation. The terminological classification of kin and affines falls into line with this scheme. Apparent anomalies in the ethnographic data are resolved if the kinship nomenclature is related to the patterns of local distribution that result from the developmental cycle of the domestic group.

It might be thought that the hypotheses from which Dr Leach starts his analysis follow as readily from the conventional notion of the life cycle of the individual as from our concept of the developmental cycle of the domestic group. I doubt this and shall try to explain why.

Let us go back to the distinction between the domain of domestic relations and the domain of politico-jural relations. In primitive societies the domain of domestic relations is commonly organized around a nucleus consisting of a mother and her children. Where the conjugal relationship and patri-filiation are jurally or ritually effective in establishing a child's jural status, the husband-father becomes a critical link between the matricentral cell and the domestic domain as a whole. In this case the elementary family may be regarded as the nucleus. This is the reproductive nucleus of the domestic domain. It consists of two, and only two, successive generations bound together by the primary dependence of the child on its parents for nurture and love and of the parents on the child as the link between them and their reproductive fulfilment. The domestic group, on the other hand, often includes three successive generations as well as members collaterally, or otherwise, linked with the nucleus of the group. In this domain, kinship, descent and other jural and affectional bonds (e.g. of adoption or slavery) enter into the constitution of the group, whereas the nucleus is formed purely by the direct bonds of marriage, filiation and siblingship. The domestic group is essentially a householding and housekeeping unit organized to provide the material and cultural resources needed to maintain and bring up its members. The distinction, as I have said before, is an analytical one. The actual composition of the

8

nuclear family and the domestic group may be identical, as it generally is in our own society; but the strictly reproductive functions, in the sense given to our concept of social reproduction, are distinguishable from the activities concerned with the production of food and shelter and the non-material means for ensuring continuity with society at large. One might put it that the domestic domain is the system of social relations through which the reproductive nucleus is integrated with the environment and with the structure of the total society.

If we consider a person's life cycle in the context of the domestic group and its development, we can distinguish four major phases in the period between his birth and his attainment of jural adulthood. In the first he is wholly contained within the matricentral cell. He is virtually merged with his mother, being no more than an appendage to her in the social and affective as well as the physiological sense. He is related to the total society only through her. This phase may last for only the few days of post-partum seclusion and may be ritually terminated, or it may merge imperceptibly into the second phase. In this the child is accepted into the patricentral nuclear family unit and his father assumes responsibility for him in relation to society and to spiritual powers. Or rather, the husband-father assumes responsibility for the mother-and-child as a unit. Presently, in the paradigmatic case, after weaning and with the acquisition of the ability to walk, he enters the third phase. He now moves into the domain of the domestic group. The spatial correlate of this phase is that the child is no longer confined to his mother's quarters but has the freedom of the whole dwelling house. He now comes under the jural and ritual care of the head of the domestic group, who may or may not be his own parent. This is the phase of childhood proper and may last for some years. During the whole of it he has no autonomous rights over property or productive resources, not even his own developing skills, no independent access to ritual institutions, and no political or jural standing in his own right. Finally he is admitted to the politico-jural domain. This confers on him actual or potential autonomy in the control of some productive resources, the elements of jural independence, rights of access to ritual powers and institutions, and some rights and duties of citizenship, as in warfare or feud. It is common for this phase to be legitimized by *rites de passage*, and to have a spatial correlate, as with the Trobriand boy who takes up residence with his maternal uncle. The culmination of the fourth phase is marriage and the actual or incipient fission of the natal domestic group.

What I am stressing in this paradigm is the changing structural relationships that make up the framework of a person's life-cycle. The stages of physiological maturation that accompany this development are of secondary significance. They are chiefly important as signs of readiness for a shift from one phase to the next. For each phase has its appropriate norms and activities connected with the basic psycho-physical capacities and needs. In the first phase a child is wholly dependent on the mother's breast for food and her arms for shelter and love. In the next phase he usually eats with his mother, sleeps in her room, and learns from her the fundamental self-oriented skills and values involved in walking, talking, feeding and cleanliness. He is regarded as sexually neutral and morally irresponsible. This pattern persists through the second phase. In the third phase the sexual division of roles and activities becomes effective. Boys are attached to their fathers and girls to their mothers. A boy commonly eats with his father or older brothers, sleeps with them, and learns objectively oriented social and economic skills and values from them. Moral responsibility is demanded of both sexes. They have to learn to control their affective attitudes to conform to customary norms of conduct and, in particular, they become subject to the incest taboos. In the next phase boys and girls eat and sleep with their like-sex age mates or peers. They are expected to take a responsible part in the performance of economic, military, jural and ritual duties for the benefit of the total society. They become answerable, to a greater or lesser degree, for moral and jural misdemeanours. Above all, they are now permitted to enter into relationships which involve adult sexuality for procreative ends, as opposed to childish sexuality for pleasurable ends. They are subject not only to the incest rules, which belong to the domestic domain, but also to the marriage regulations, which emanate from the politico-jural domain. *Rites de passage* often serve to dramatize this fact.

Though these phases do not invariably conform to stages of physiological growth, in relatively homogeneous social systems there is a close parallelism between them. For in such societies the basic educational tasks required to produce an adult person capable of playing a full part in maintaining and transmitting the social capital seem to be complete at about the same time as the attainment of physical and sexual maturity and therewith the capacity for replacing the parental generation in productive and reproductive activities. But what I want particularly to emphasize is that the maturation of the individual and his proper passage through the life cycle is of paramount concern to society at large. This is shown in the widespread occurrence of institutionalized procedures for legitimizing each step in it, and especially for terminating the period of jural infancy, whether it ends with adolescence or extends into the stage of physical adulthood.

Initiation, puberty and nubility ceremonies are the most dramatic instances of such procedures. They do not come into our symposium but a brief reference to them will help to bring home my argument. In these ceremonies the domestic group's task of social reproduction is terminated. Having bred, reared and educated the child, it hands over the finished product to the total society. It is a transaction in which the power and authority of the politico-jural order as the final arbiter over the human and social capital of society are asserted. It is a situation in which the distinctive interests of the domestic group and those of the total society are liable to clash. In their capacity as citizens, parents wish their children to be admitted to the politico-jural domain and to have the rights of jural adulthood conferred on them. But as parents they may fear and resent having to relinquish their children to the superior and impersonal powers of society at large. Their resistance may be strengthened by the knowledge that initiation is the thin end of the wedge that will ultimately split the family. The children for their part, however mature they are and however much they value admission to adulthood, may hesitate to step out of the protective circle of the home. It may be particularly hard to renounce the bond of primal dependency on the mother which goes back to the first phase of the life cycle. If there is a marked cleavage between the domestic domain and the politico-jural domain these resistances may be institutionalized and the more difficult to overcome. Hence society may have to use harsh and abrupt rites to tear the new citizen away from his natal family and to assert its right to incorporate him as an adult. Citizenship may need a drastic reorientation of moral values and of social and economic roles in the new recruit. Shock tactics may be the readiest way to bring this about. Furthermore, the stamp of legitimacy must be publicly and incontrovertibly set upon the new rights (notably those of jural autonomy and procreative sexuality)—and corresponding duties (notably those defending the social order against dangers from within, such as crime, and against the external dangers of war and feud)—which are conferred by citizenship.

I am not here concerned with the theory of initiation ceremonies and further discussion of them would be out of place. I have referred to them merely in order to illustrate what I mean by a movement or transaction between the two domains of social structure we have been analysing. There are many societies in which the movement is not legitimized by means of initiation or other ceremonies. The reason may be that the two domains are not, analytically speaking, separated by a decisive cleavage. In any case, the movement does take place. There is a phase in the life cycle when jural infancy draws to an end and jural adulthood begins. It may be initiated, as has already been suggested, by marriage or by the birth of a couple's first child. Initiation ceremonies, in the strict sense, are often regarded as the prelude to marriage, if they do not actually end in marriage. In general, what finally terminates jural infancy is the emergence of the family nucleus for the new domestic group that is destined to replace that of the parents. Initiation ceremonies are sometimes spread over months or years, the preliminary rites serving, as it were, to apprentice the new recruit to the politico-jural domain and the later ones serving to make him free of that domain when he has proved worthy. Analogously, institutions like the shift of residence at adolescence from the father's to the maternal uncle's house may be regarded as the first steps in a longer process of jural emancipation which ends with marriage.

One consideration that must not be lost sight of is the reciprocal relationship between the two domains. Every member of a society is simultaneously a person in the domestic domain and in the politico-jural domain. His status in the former receives definition and sanction from the latter. Jural infancy is structurally located in the domestic domain, but its character is defined by norms validated in the politico-jural domain. Take the extreme case of an Ashanti infant which is defined as being non-human, that is, not a potential member of society, if it dies before the naming ceremony on the eighth day after its birth. This jural status derives from the politico-jural domain. The parents are obliged to accept the definition whatever their private emotions may be.

This has a direct bearing on the internal structure of the domestic group. The differentials in this structure are in part inherent in the procreative relationship and spring from the requirements of child rearing. But their character is also decisively regulated by politico-jural norms. The gap between successive generations can be large or small, varying with the kind and degree of authority and power vested in the parental generation; solidarity can be stressed more than rivalry in the sibling group, as in lineage systems, or vice versa, as among the Iban. These are differences of magnitude and of precedence related to the balance that is struck in a particular social system between the variables that combine together in the organization of the domestic domain. They are expressed in customs, beliefs and institutions that are the collective possessions of the whole society not the private culture of each domestic group.

The classical illustration is the contrast in the relationships of fathers and children in patrilineal and in matrilineal descent systems. Dr Goody's paper brings this out with new effect. It is because the father is not vested with jural authority over his son and the son has no title to the inheritance of his father's properties or to succession to his offices and rank, that matrilineal fathers and sons have an affectionate, non-competitive relationship. Conversely, it is because maternal uncles have jurally sanctioned rights over their nephews and the latter have jurally sanctioned claims on their uncles that there is tension in their relationship. And the pattern is reversed in patrilineal systems because the locus of rights and claims is jurally reversed. Matrilineal fatherhood is defined as primarily a domestic relationship with only a minimal function in the politico-jural domain. Hence its focus is the task of bringing up and educating a child and fathers must rely on moral and affectional sanctions to fulfil it. In the last resort society will stand behind them to prevent trespass on their prerogative but gives them no support in the enforcement of their will on their children. We can contrast this with the juridical support society gives to the matrilineal husband in enforcing his rights to the sexual services of his wife. A patrilineal father, on the other hand, has not only the domestic and parental roles of provider and educator. He also has rights enforceable by juridical sanctions over and towards them and they have corresponding claims on him. He represents the power of society as a force within the domestic group in a way that the matrilineal father does not. And this analysis could be carried further if we were to take into consideration a third domain of social structure, that of ritual institutions. I have made allusions to this domain but it is not directly pertinent to our inquiries.

This formulation enables us to see why numerical data are essential for the analysis of the developmental cycle of the domestic group. Each phase of the cycle can be thought of as the outcome of a set of 'pushes' and 'pulls', antecedent and contemporaneous. They come in part from within the domestic domain and in part from the external structure of society. Numerical data provide a means of assessing the relative strength of these forces and of describing their configuration at a given phase. The papers that make up our symposium give ample confirmation of this argument, notably Dr Freeman's. It is hard to see how he could have reached his conclusions without numerical data. But let us take a simpler case such as we find in a society like the Tallensi, with their rigorous patrilineal descent system. During the expansion phase of the domestic group all forces converge on supporting the paramountcy of the father in the domestic domain. He controls all the productive resources required to provide for his wife and children and he is vested with jural authority over them. Neither his wife nor his children have jural status, economic rights or ritual standing except through him. Consistently with this a man's wife, and his children during their jural infancy, can be expected to live with him, and numerical data show that they invariably do so. In the dispersion phase, however, a son's rights to some measure of jural, economic and ritual independence become operative, and he may set up his own dwelling group. But whether he moves out of the parental home altogether to farm on his own or remains residentially attached to his father's homestead depends on factors internal to the domestic group. If he is the only son he will be less likely to move away than if he has brothers and if he is the oldest son he will be more likely to do so than if he is a younger son. Moreover the move may take place by stages and will not be complete until he has young children of his own. Numerical data are essential to assess the relative weight of these factors; and it has now become an established practice among social anthropologists to use such data in the analysis of social structure. Outstanding recent examples are the studies by Dr Raymond T. Smith, Professor J. Clyde Mitchell and the late Dr David Tait. They are specially pertinent to the present context because they all utilize the developmental cycle of the domestic group as their framework of analysis.

INTRODUCTION

REFERENCES CITED

Goodenough, Ward H. 'Residence Rules', *Southwestern Journal of Anthropology*, 12, 1, 1956.

Smith, Raymond T. *The Negro Family in British Guiana: family structure and social status in the villages.* (London, 1956.)

Mitchell, J. Clyde. *The Yao Village: a Study in the Social Structure of a Nyasaland Tribe.* (Published for the Rhodes-Livingstone Institute by the Manchester University Prèss, 1956.)

Tait, David. 'The Family, Household and Minor Lineage of the Konkomba', *Africa*, vol. XXVI, no. 3, July 1956 and no. 4, October 1956.

THE FAMILY SYSTEM OF THE
IBAN OF BORNEO

By J. D. FREEMAN

INTRODUCTION

The Iban [1]—with whose family system this essay is concerned—are a people of western Borneo. They are to be found, for the most part, among the remote, jungle-covered ranges of the undeveloped interior zone of Sarawak, and also in certain of the inaccessible headwaters of the great Kapuas river, in what is now Kalimantan or Indonesian Borneo.

In the judgement of A. C. Haddon, the Iban are Oceanic Mongols, and they belong to an ethnic stock which he has termed Proto-Malay (Haddon and Start 1936: 1). In brief, they are a brachycephalic people (average c.i. 83), of short stature (average height of males, 5 ft. 2½ in.), with lank, black hair, cinnamon coloured skins, and typically Mongoloid features.

Iban culture is also fundamentally proto-Malayan in type. In particular, the Iban language has many close affinities with Malay, and Howell, a leading authority, classes Iban as 'a dialect of the wide spreading Malay language'. The Iban language has not, however, been influenced by Arabic; nor have Iban culture and social institutions been appreciably affected by Islam.

In Sarawak today, the Iban are the predominant element in a highly heterogeneous population. The total population of Sarawak as disclosed by the census of 1947 was 546,385, and of this number 190,326 (or 34·8 %) were Iban. Sarawak, like so many of the other countries of south-east Asia, has a plural society. Along the coast, among the deltaic swamps and in the low-lying country bordering the tidal reaches of the rivers, one finds the main centres of Malay, Chinese and Melanau settlement. Further inland, amid steep and tangled ranges drained by swift-flowing streams and rivers, live the indigenous hill peoples: the Land Dayaks, the Iban, the Kayan, the Kenyah, the Kajang and others, all of them with subsistence economies based on the shifting cultivation of dry rice.

In particular, this essay is concerned with the Ulu Ai Iban of the Baleh river of the Third Division of Sarawak. The Baleh enters the great Rejang river, from the west, at a point about 170 river miles from the sea, and along its banks and those of its numerous tributaries (the Sut, Mujong, Gat and Merirai being the most important of them), there are scattered some 133 Iban communities with a total population of about 11,500. Almost all of these

15

people are the descendants of migrants from the interior of the Second Division of Sarawak, and especially from the headwaters of the Batang.Lupar. Travelling chiefly by way of the Katibas and Ngemah rivers, the first of these migrants reached the primeval forests of the Baleh in the early 1880's, but it was not until about forty years later, following serious conflict with the Brooke Government, that permanent Iban settlement was achieved[2]. Today the Baleh is an exclusively Iban area.

During the years—from 1949 to 1951—when my field research was undertaken[3], the Iban of the Baleh region were still little touched by the outside world. Their men, with long hair and bodies profusely tattooed, and their women, clad in ikat skirts of their own weaving, were all still pagan and pre-literate; and throughout the whole Baleh region, Iban culture—in all its extraordinary richness—was still a flourishing reality. In this essay then, we shall be concerned with the traditional ways of the Iban, ways which—because of the tolerant policies of the White Rajahs of Sarawak—have survived unscathed into the modern world.

THE IBAN LONG-HOUSE

All of the Iban of the Baleh region still live in long-houses. Architecturally there is nothing very remarkable about an Iban long-house, but many of them, out of sheer length, make an impressive spectacle. Rumah Tungku, for example, one of the long-houses selected for detailed discussion in this essay, extends in an uninterrupted line for more than a sixth of a mile. Standing on an elevated terrace, well beyond the reach of flood waters, and lifted high on score upon score of hardwood piles, it stretches—as do all Iban long-houses—along the bank of a river. Here and there, entry ladders of notched logs lead up like gangways to the *tanju*, an open platform that runs the entire length of the spindly structure and gives access to the public gallery and the family apartments beyond. Over both gallery and apartments a low-pitched roof of wooden shingles forms an unbroken expanse. At first glance the whole sprawling building seems like some huge barracks or pavilion.

Few long-houses have the dimensions of Rumah Tungku (sixty to a hundred yards is more common a length), but, casually regarded, all Iban long-houses do have the appearance of being compact architectural units, and this appearance has led some writers (Baring-Gould and Bampfylde 1909: 27) to the supposition that the long-house is therefore the outcome of some kind of communal or group organization and ownership. For the Iban, however, this supposition is very far from the truth.

Although the platform (*tanju*) and the gallery (*ruai*) of a long-house do extend without interruption throughout its entire length, an Iban long-house is, in fact, made up of a series of independently owned apartments, and

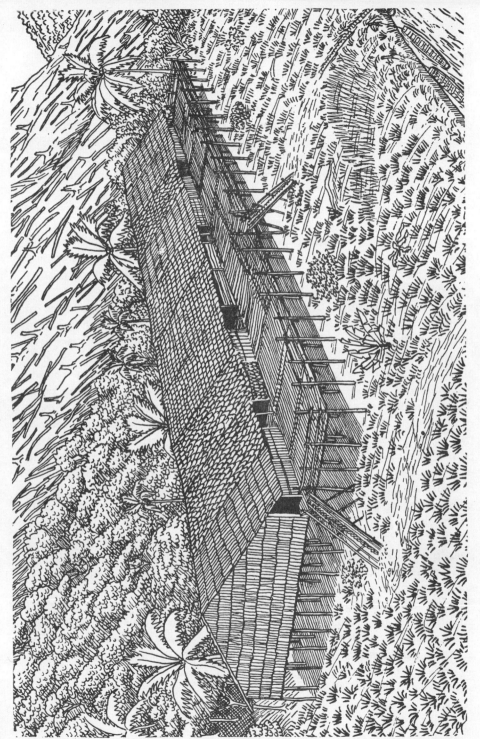

Fig. 1. An Iban long-house

further, these apartments, although joined one to the other architecturally, are always the separate abodes of distinct and autonomous family groups. Indeed, the only parts of the whole long-house which are held in any sort of common ownership are the entry ladders; for the rest, every pile and every plank is privately owned by one of the community's component families. In a sense, then, the singular architecture of an Iban long-house is deceptive, for its gallery and its unbroken expanse of roof tend to cloak the fact that it is made up of a series of separate apartments, each of which is the property of a sovereign family group.

Among the various families which make up a long-house community there does always exist a network of relationships based on bilateral kinship. Thus, every family is always related cognatically to at least one of the other families of the community, usually to several, and quite often to many of them. However, it rarely, if ever, occurs that there is within a long-house community a degree of complete, or even nearly complete, inter-relatedness among its various family groups. Furthermore, an Iban long-house community is an open and not a closed group, for its component family groups are joined in free association from which withdrawal is always possible, and there is, indeed, a good deal of movement, year by year, from one long-house to another. As all this suggests, an Iban long-house community is a corporate group only in certain restricted ways. Thus a long-house community holds virtually no property in common ownership, nor is there collective ownership of farm land; and again, there is an absence of any kind of economic activity by the long-house as a corporate group. However, membership of a long-house does impose upon each family group many common duties and obligations, for it is universally accepted that the well-being of any long-house is dependent upon its ritual state, and for the maintaining of this all are responsible. In jural matters also the long-house community is a corporate entity, for all its family groups do place themselves under the jurisdiction of their *tuai rumah*, or house headman, whose principal duty is the safe-guarding and administering of the customary law, or *adat*.

As these summary remarks suggest, the Iban long-house community, as such, presents a number of sociological problems of extraordinary interest. These problems I hope, in due time, to discuss, but in the present essay our attention will be confined to the independent family cells of which every long-house community is composed. Of these it may be claimed that they are the intrinsic and irreducible corporate groups of Iban society, and certainly, an understanding of them is an essential preliminary to the study of the wider structure of Iban society.

THE FAMILY SYSTEM OF THE IBAN OF BORNEO

THE FAMILY APARTMENT

While they may vary slightly in width, all of the separate family apartments of an Iban long-house are basically similar in construction. Each apartment always consists of a single walled room (with an attic above it), a section of the roofed gallery, and a division of the open platform which fronts the whole house. Of these, the walled room or *bilek* is by far the most important. First and foremost the *bilek* is the family parlour: the normal location for cooking, eating, sleeping, and a host of domestic tasks. But not only is the *bilek* the setting for a family's mundane life, it is also the place where all of its valued heirloom property is displayed or stored. At the back of each parlour stands the family's collection of *tajau*—massive pottery jars, usually of Chinese manufacture, one or other of which, because of its great age, may have become an object of religious veneration. Stacked in the corners or suspended from the side walls is the family's bronze ware: gongs of many shapes and sizes, trays and boxes for use in the ceremony of betel chewing, and perhaps a Malay cannon or two. Other family possessions, less durable and more rarely used, resplendent *ikat* fabrics, the silver jewellery and bead garments of the women, the feather head-dresses and traditional accoutrements of the men, are securely stored away and only brought out on ritual or gala occasions. All of these valuables make up an important part of the family estate.

Ranged along the back of the long-house, then, are a series of family rooms, each divided from its neighbour by a side wall of planks or bark. Each of these rooms is connected by a hinged door (which may be barred from within) to the great gallery (*ruai*) of the long-house, which serves as a kind of general thoroughfare and is the principal venue of the community's social and ritual life. Of this gallery each family possesses its own section, and although the whole of the *ruai* is ordinarily open to all members of the long-house, each family retains the prescriptive right to cordon off its own part whenever, for ritual reasons, the need arises. Here and there, in about the centre of the *ruai*, in smoke-blackened clusters, hang the trophy heads or *antu pala*, with which so many of the most cherished values and beliefs of the Iban are associated. But each cluster is always the private property of the family on whose section of the gallery it hangs, for trophy heads are never owned by the long-house as a whole.

From each family division of the gallery an opening gives access to the open platform, or *tanju*, which like the *ruai* runs from end to end of the long-house, providing a space where rice may be sunned and garments dried. Of this platform, too, each family possesses its own portion.

Each family then, owns and occupies a single apartment (made up of a *bilek*, a *ruai*, and a *tanju*), and it is the joining together of a series of these distinct apartments that produces the attenuated structure known as a long-house. In other words, a long-house is, in essence, a 'village' consisting of a single terrace of attached houses.

In government and other publications the family apartments of an Iban long-house are commonly referred to as 'doors'. A long-house, that is, is referred to as consisting of ten doors, twenty doors, or whatever the number may be. This method of description has the advantage that it may be applied to any of the indigenous peoples of Borneo that live in long-houses; but in this essay—which is concerned exclusively with the Iban—I propose to employ the term *bilek*. As we have seen, *bilek* is the word which the Iban use to describe the separate enclosed rooms of a long-house, but it is also the term used, by the Iban themselves, to refer to the family group which owns and occupies one apartment of a long-house, as—for example—in the phrases: '*Nya prau kami se bilek*' ('That is the canoe of our *bilek*, or family'), and '*Kami se bilek tabin magang*' ('We, of this *bilek* family, are all ill'). The family group denoted in the phrase '*kami se bilek*'[4] ('we, the members of a *bilek*') is the basic unit of Iban social and economic organization. In the discussion that follows, I shall refer to this unit as the *bilek* family.

The members of a *bilek* family are always intimately related by ties of kinship and affinity, but it is a unit which is primarily defined by the criterion of local residence. Its members—as a group—own and occupy one, and only one, of the separate apartments of a long-house, consisting, as already described, of a walled room, a section of roofed gallery and of open platform. A *bilek* family is always, therefore, a local group.

Further, the *bilek* family is always a domestic family; that is, its members constitute a single household, and each household subsists as an autonomous unit. Food is prepared and cooked for the *bilek* family as a whole, and its members eat together, sharing a common meal. The *bilek* family is also an allodial unit, possessing both land and property in its own right. Thus, a *bilek* family always owns tracts of rice-land, in various parts of the hilly terrain surrounding the long-house, over which it has established rights by the felling of virgin jungle. And, if the settlement be an old one, each family will also possess scattered clumps of durian and other fruit trees, thickets of rattan, and perhaps a small rubber plantation. Again, in addition to its dug-out canoe, its domestic and agricultural tools and paraphernalia, each family will always have its own assemblage of *tajau*, *tawak* and other heirloom valuables. Similarly, each *bilek* family is an independent entity economically, cultivating its own hill rice, growing or collecting a wide range of supplementary food crops, and producing—as best it can—all the other necessaries of existence. Ritually too, each *bilek* family is a disparate unit with its own magical charms (*pengaroh*), its own set of ritual prohibitions (*pemali*), and its own special kind of sacred rice (*padi pun*). Finally, almost all of the *gawai*

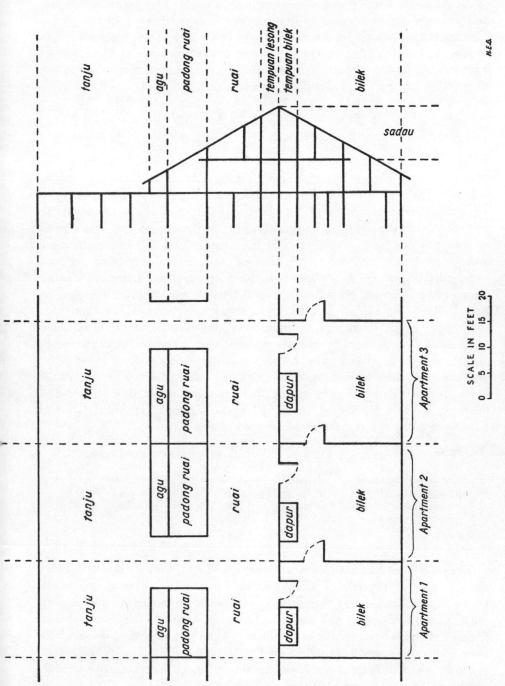

SCALE IN FEET

0 5 10 15 20

Fig. 2. Plan of an Iban long-house.

21

of the Iban—elaborate rituals aimed at the acquisition of longevity, prosperity and prestige—are performed by independent *bilek* families.

Among the Iban there are no clans or other large-scale, corporate, kin groups, and so the *bilek* family is a social unit of primary and paramount importance. As one highly intelligent Iban[5] phrased it: 'Each *bilek* is like a sovereign country' ('*Bilek siti, baka menoa siti*').

REPRESENTATIVE SAMPLING AND QUANTITATIVE ANALYSIS

Before turning to detailed discussion of the characteristics of the Iban *bilek* family, I should like to comment briefly on the data upon which my analysis is based. During the period of my field research the Baleh region contained 133 long-house communities, with a total population of about 11,500. After an extensive reconnaissance, Rumah Nyala[6], in the Sungai Sut, was chosen as a site for intensive investigation of Iban methods of hill rice cultivation, and an apartment, built on to the *tanju* of Rumah Nyala, became our base camp for the two years we spent in the Baleh region. Later, two other communities—Rumah Sibat, of Sungai Melinau, and Rumah Tungku, of Sungai Tiau—were also selected for detailed study, and more than four months were spent working in these two long-houses. Many additional communities were visited for shorter periods; thus, we stayed at twelve other long-houses for periods varying from two or three days to over a fortnight, and brief day visits were made to about twenty other Iban settlements in the Baleh region. For the purposes of the analysis presented in this essay, however, the *bilek* families of the three long-houses most intensively studied have been taken as a representative sample. These were:

Name of long-house	Total number of *bilek* families in long-house	Total number of members of long-house
Rumah Nyala	25	140
Rumah Sibat	32	172
Rumah Tungku	50	303
Totals	107	615

The quantitative and other evidence presented in this essay is based, then, on a sample of 107 *bilek* families drawn from three different long-house communities. These three communities, it should be remarked, are discrete entities both territorially and socially. However, although they were chosen for considerations extraneous to the theme of the present essay, it cannot be claimed that they provide us with a random selection of families. Nonetheless, it can be asserted that our 107 *bilek* families do form a representative sample, pertinent for our present inquiries.

Throughout the Baleh region there is marked cultural and social homogeneity; in none of the many other Baleh communities which I reconnoitred was there any significant divergence from the main regularities and principles established by the analysis of the 107 *bilek* families of our sample, and I have no hesitation in coming to the conclusion that the general findings of this essay are applicable to the Baleh region as a whole. Indeed, from my observations among the Iban of the Rejang, the Katibas, the Saribas and the Ulu Batang Ai and several other rivers of the Second and Third Divisions, there is good reason to suppose that the family system described in this essay is the family system of all the Iban tribes of Sarawak.

THE BILEK FAMILY

The Iban *bilek* family has two dominant characteristics: it is a small group numerically, and a simple one genealogically. Table 1 shows the range in numerical composition of all the *bilek* families of the three long-houses of our sample.

Table 1. *Numerical composition of the 'bilek' family*

Number of persons in bilek family	2	3	4	5	6	7	8	9	10	11	12	13	14
Frequency													
Rumah Nyala	–	7	3	4	3	2	2	1	3	–	–	–	–
Rumah Sibat	3	2	7	4	9	4	–	–	3	–	–	–	–
Rumah Tungku	2	4	9	9	6	7	7	1	3	–	1	–	1
Totals	5	13	19	17	18	13	9	2	9	–	1	–	1

It will be seen that eighty of the 107 *bilek* families of the sample—that is, approximately 75%—fall within the range of from three to seven members per family. The mode is four, and the median five persons per *bilek*; while the arithmetical mean is 5·75 persons per *bilek*, with a mean deviation of 1·8. This accords closely with other data available for the Baleh region[7]. When it is realized that the *bilek* family is the basic unit in agriculture as in almost all other activities, it will become apparent that its limited size is a factor of crucial importance in all economic pursuits. Similarly, it is a feature of cardinal sociological significance.

Now, while it is true that the *bilek* family is, in general, a small group numerically, an inspection of Table 1 will indicate that families do show a not inconsiderable range in size. This variation results from the fact that our sample includes *bilek* families at several different stages of development, from households consisting of a single married couple at one extreme to those which extend through four consecutive generations at the other.

23

In Table 2 the 107 *bilek* families of our sample have been classifi**é**d according to the number of generations they contain, and for each category the main type of genealogical composition has been shown.

Table *2*. *Genealogical composition of the 'bilek' family*

Number of generations in *bilek* family	Frequency	Approximate percentage of sample	Main type of genealogical composition
1	3	3%	Married couple, without children
2	43	40%	Parents with children
3	51	48%	Grandparents, child and spouse, and grandchildren
4	10	9%	Great-grandparent, child and spouse, grandchild and spouse, and great-grandchildren

It will be observed that some of the *bilek* families listed in Table 2 (i.e. those comprising two generations) are simple elementary families, but all of these are at an interjacent stage of development, and all of them—in the normal course of events—are likely to grow into three-generation families. This brings us to one of the prime features of the Iban family system.

Among the Iban, *at least one* of the children of a family, when he or she reaches maturity and marries, remains in the parents' *bilek*. All of the other children of the family may marry out, and so become members of other units, but one always stays in the natal *bilek*. In this way the Iban *bilek* family achieves a continuity through time as, from one generation to the next, one elementary family grows out of and succeeds another in an unbroken sequence.[8] This means that, in theory, every Iban *bilek* family is a perennial corporate group. In other words, although birth, adoption, marriage and death do result in regular changes in its personnel, a *bilek* does persist through time as a clearly defined entity: an estate in land and property which, at any moment, is always held in common ownership by a group of co-existing family members.

Normally, an Iban *bilek* family contains three generations, consisting, for example, of a pair of grandparents, a son or daughter and his or her spouse, and their grandchildren. The average size of families of this type is about seven members. Sometimes, four-generation families come into being, but *bileks* of this type are not common, occurring in only about 9% of cases, and almost all of them are brought about by the greater longevity of women. Three-generation *bileks* are much more usual, about 48% of families being of this type.

If a *bilek* family contains fewer than three generations this state of affairs has always been brought about in one of two ways: either by process of death, or by process of *bilek* partition. The first of these is self-explanatory: if all the members of the grandparent generation of a *bilek* family are removed by death, a three-generation family thus becomes a two-generation family. Partition (presently to be discussed in detail) is the process whereby a sibling secedes from his (or her) natal *bilek* to set up an independent family unit. It is a common occurrence in Iban society. The seceding group is almost always an elementary family (e.g. a sibling, his spouse and their children), though occasionally it may consist of a married couple without children. Further, for a seceding group to contain more than two generations is an exceedingly rare event.

Now, of our sample of 107 *bilek* families, forty-six (or about 43%) were groups of only one or two generations, the average size of the two-generation families being about four members. An examination of the recent histories of these forty-six *bilek* families shows that twenty-one of them have been brought into being by the death of members of the grandparent generation, so reducing them to two-generation groups, while twenty-five are cases of newly established families brought about by process of partition. In the normal course of events all of these forty-six one- and two-generation families will grow (by process of marriage and birth) into three-generation families.

The *bilek* family then is simple in its structure for it is essentially based on a direct extension of the elementary family. Iban society—as will have become apparent—is rigorously monogamous, and so there are no compound families. Again, the development of laterally extended families is precluded by a strong tendency towards partition as soon as a *bilek* family increases in size and collateral elementary families begin to emerge. Thus, in the three long-houses under discussion, there was not a single instance of married siblings both possessing adult children and yet still living together as members of the same *bilek* family. Nor did I encounter an instance of this in Iban communities in other parts of Sarawak.

BILEK FAMILY MEMBERSHIP

We have now seen that the Iban *bilek* family is an autonomous group of limited size and of simple genealogical structure. It is well possible, therefore, to define in fairly precise terms the various processes whereby a *bilek* family normally increases or—conversely—diminishes its membership. These processes are summarized in Table 3. In the discussion that follows, the most important of these processes will be reviewed.

We may begin by examining the principles of recruitment to *bilek* family membership. At any given time, any Iban man, woman or child is a resident member of one *bilek*, and one *bilek* only. He (or she) may have gained

Table 3. *The 'bilek' family*

Processes whereby the personnel of a *bilek* family may be increased	Processes whereby the personnel of a *bilek* family may be diminished
1. By the birth of a child	1. By the death of a member
2. By the adoption of a child from another *bilek* family	2. By one of its members being adopted into another *bilek* family
3. By an individual marrying into the *bilek* (possibly with children by a previous union)	3. By a member marrying out into another *bilek* (possibly with children by a previous union)
4. By the return of an out-marrying member after divorce (possibly accompanied by children)	4. By the return of an affine to his (or her) natal *bilek* after divorce (possibly accompanied by children)
5. By amalgamation with another *bilek* family	5. By partition: the secession of some members to set up a new and independent *bilek* family

membership of this *bilek* in one of three main ways: by having been born into it, by having been adopted into it, or by having married into it. In Table 4, the 615 members of the 107 *bilek* families of Rumah Nyala, Rumah Sibat and Rumah Tungku, have been classified under these three headings.

Table 4. *Recruitment to 'bilek' family membership*

Principle of recruitment to *bilek* family	Number of individuals	Percentage of total
Birth	418	67·9
Adoption	53	8·6
Marriage	144	23·3

Let us now glance at these different principles of recruitment.

RECRUITMENT BY BIRTH: THE PRINCIPLE OF UTROLATERAL FILIATION

Every individual in Iban society is born into one particular *bilek*, and this is just as likely to be the *bilek* of the child's father as it is to be the *bilek* of the child's mother, for virilocal residence and uxorilocal residence occur with very nearly equal incidence. An analysis of an extensive series of Iban marriages, for all of which reliable information was available, shows that virilocal residence occurred in 49 % of cases as against uxorilocal residence in 51 % of cases. In other words, among the Iban marriage is *utrolocal*: that is, there is a system of marriage in which *either* virilocal *or* uxorilocal residence may be followed and in which rules of kinship and inheritance result in neither form of domicile being given any special kind of preference.

The *bilek* family of which a child is a member by right of birth, and in which he (or she) grows up, we may term his (or her) *natal bilek*. It is to this *bilek*—and this *bilek* alone—that he belongs, and he remains a member of it for the whole of his life, unless he be adopted, or, upon reaching adulthood, marries out into some other *bilek* family.

Further, membership of his (or her) natal *bilek* confers upon a child inheritance rights over its properties and lands, and these rights are retained as long as the individual remains a resident member. Among the Iban, then, filiation [9] is of a special kind, for it may be either to an individual's mother's *bilek* or to an individual's father's *bilek*, but not to both at the same time. Moreover, in practice, both types of filiation occur to an approximately equal extent. We are here confronted with a fundamental principle of the Iban family system.

To the best of my knowledge no precisely similar system of filiation has hitherto been recorded, and it becomes necessary, therefore, to introduce a new term to describe its special characteristics.

After much consideration I have decided that the best term to apply to the type of filiation found among the Iban is *utrolateral*. [10] This term has the merit that it clearly points to the fact that one side or the other is always chosen, but never both; and this is the very principle which we are wanting to define and accentuate.

By the term *utrolateral*, then, I mean to denote a system of filiation in which an individual can possess membership of either his father's or his mother's birth group (i.e. the *bilek* family among the Iban), but not of both at the same time.

It will be noted that two clearly distinct criteria are implicit in this formulation: (i) the criterion of descent, and (ii) the criterion of local residence. In theory, each child is, by birth, eligible for membership of either his father's or his mother's *bilek* family, but the necessity of a single place of local residence means that, in practice, he becomes a member of only one of these two groups. And, in any given instance, it is the type of marital domicile (either virilocal or uxorilocal) followed by the parents that determines the *bilek* family to which a child actually belongs. In short, it is filial consanguinity and local residence acting together which establish the status of the natal members of any *bilek* family.

A child, we have asserted, is just as likely, under the Iban system of filiation, to be a member of his father's birth group as he is to be a member of his mother's birth group. Evidence for this assertion is contained in Table 5. This Table has reference to *bilek* families in which there is a married couple with one or more children under twenty years of age born of their union. All such cases in the three long-houses Rumah Nyala, Rumah Sibat and Rumah Tungku are included.

Table 5. '*Bilek*' family filiation

Name of long-house	*Bilek* families in which children are living as members of their mother's birth group	*Bilek* families in which children are living as members of their father's birth group
Rumah Nyala	6	13
Rumah Sibat	10	9
Rumah Tungku	16	7
Totals	32	29

All of the household appearing in this Table were visited, and observed at first hand, during the years 1949–50. The even balancing of the two types of filiation is clearly apparent: apartments in which children are living as members of their mother's *bilek* family make up approximately 52 % of the total, while those in which children are living as members of their father's *bilek* family comprise about 48 %. This leads us to the general observation that, under the Iban family system, maternal and paternal filiation occur with virtually equal incidence, and that both kinds of filiation have the same jural and structural significance.

ADOPTION

We have now delineated the principles of filiation which hold for the natal members of a *bilek* family; exactly the same principles apply to adopted individuals. Furthermore, under Iban *adat*, an adopted child has conferred upon him precisely the same rights within his new *bilek* family as have those who are born members; and the public discussion which accompanies formal adoption is always chiefly concerned with the reiteration and exemplification of this basic rule. The occasion is also marked by ritual observances[11] which are a graphic symbolic expression of the fact that adoption involves the cessation of membership rights in the child's natal apartment and the assumption of exactly similar rights in his adoptive *bilek* family.

Adoption is widely prevalent in Iban society, occurring in about one-third of all apartments. Thus, the fifty-three cases of adoption (recorded in Table 4) were distributed in thirty-nine (or about 36 %) of the *bilek* families of our sample.

The reasons for this heavy incidence of adoption are to be sought partly in demographic factors, and partly in the jural character of the *bilek* family. Among the Iban the marriage rate is extremely high. Indeed, from my observations in the Baleh region, it can be said that all normal individuals become married at some stage of their lives, though for a not inconsiderable proportion a state of permanent divorce eventually ensues. However, despite this high marriage rate, childless unions—resulting either from infant mortality or sterility—are fairly common. Inquiries at Rumah Nyala[12] showed an infant mortality rate (i.e. death at birth or within the first five years of life) of approximately 0·4; and from investigations carried out at all the long-houses of our sample it would appear that about 18 % of women reach menopause without having raised children of their own. [13] These are the women who, lacking issue of their own, have recourse to adoption.

Mention has already been made of the way in which an Iban family normally persists through time as an allodial unit. If this process is to continue without intermission the family must perpetuate itself; each generation must produce or acquire the children who are to inherit the *bilek* and its heirloom property in the next. It is possible for a family to fail in this task, and so become extinct. The Iban use the word *punas*, meaning 'sterile', to describe this event, as in the phrase: '*Bilek sida udah punas*' ('Their *bilek* family has become extinct'). It must not be thought, however, that the extinction of *bilek* families is a common phenomenon; on the contrary, such a happening is extremely rare, for every effort is made to avoid so ignominious a fate. In the last resort, the one or two survivors of a depleted family will seek amalgamation with some other *bilek*, but the preferred and more usual course is to augment one's dwindling family by the adoption of new members. In most cases the risk of extinction is foreseen by many years, and young children are adopted, but it does sometimes happen that adults are adopted into a family which has been stricken by disease or some other misfortune. An analysis of the fifty-three extra-*bilek* adoptions appearing in Table 4 shows that about 70 % of them had been contracted by persons having no children of their own. This percentage clearly indicates the principal motive prompting adoption.

Adoption enables childless couples to escape from their undesired predicament. Moreover, the children who are adopted, as heirs apparent, can be relied upon to care for their adoptive parents in sickness and old age, and to perform the complex mortuary rites which, in Iban eyes, are of critical importance. These duties discharged, the adopted children inherit their parents' *bilek* and all the property it contains, so ensuring its survival as an independent unit. Adoption operating in this way to save a *bilek* from extinction is a not uncommon phenomenon. Thus, of the 107 *bilek* families of Rumah Nyala, Rumah Sibat and Rumah Tungku, seventeen (or approximately 16 %) depended on an adoption for their future existence.

MARRIAGE

We have now briefly examined recruitment by birth and recruitment by adoption. Full membership of a *bilek* family may also be attained by marrying into it. Marriage, indeed, is a crucial determinant of *bilek* family membership. As already remarked, the Iban are a rigorously monogamous people, and further, the Iban *bilek* family—by *adat*—is a strictly exogamous unit. Iban custom does ordinarily permit the marriage of first cousins (*petunggal diri menyadi*), but incest rules prescribe that marriage between first cousins who are resident members of the same *bilek* should never take place. [14] From this fact that marriage never occurs within the confines of a single *bilek* family it follows that every marriage necessitates one of the partners leaving his or her natal or adoptive *bilek*.

This means that when he marries a man has two courses of action open to him: he may bring his wife to live as a member of his own natal or adoptive *bilek* (i.e. in-marriage), or he may move to the natal or adoptive *bilek* of his wife (i.e. out-marriage). A woman, when she marries, is faced with a similar choice: she may take up residence either in her own *bilek* or in that of her husband. Marriage accompanied by neolocal residence never occurs (Murdock 1949: 16–17).

The Iban have a special term to describe the act of marrying out of one's natal or adoptive family. It is the verb *ngugi* (root form: *ugi*), which Howell and Bailey translate as: 'to go and live in the husband's (or wife's) *bilek*' (Howell and Bailey 1900: 182). In the Baleh region the phrase *ngugi ka orang* is commonly used. These words meaning 'to go, on marriage, and reside with other people' (i.e. the *bilek* family of one's spouse), describe the process even more clearly. The term *ngugi* applies equally to males and females, and so to both virilocal and uxorilocal out-marriage.

Now, as already remarked, among the Iban virilocal marriage and uxorilocal marriage are equally permissible, for in Iban culture there are no beliefs or values which result in either form of marriage being given any sort of special preference. However, in all cases of permanent marriage a definite choice between the two possibilities must in the end be made, for there is no long-term system of alternate residence. Often, it is true, a newly married couple will follow first one form of domicile and then the other before finally settling down. Marrying into another apartment means permanently departing from one's natal or adoptive *bilek* family, and it is almost always an occasion of stress and sorrow, particularly for the parents of the seceding son or daughter. Conflicts of interest very frequently arise, but if a marriage is to endure a compromise is always reached, and, sooner or later, the couple permanently adopt either virilocal or uxorilocal residence.

Let us now consider the evidence for these assertions. Of the 140 affines listed in Table 4, sixty-five were men with uxorilocal domicile while seventy-five were women with virilocal domicile. In a more numerous series of marriages—284 in all, both past and present—taken from genealogies collected at Rumah Nyala, Rumah Sibat and Rumah Tungku, there were 145 instances of uxorilocal residence (or 51 % approximately) as against 139 instances (or 49% approximately) of virilocal residence. These evenly balanced percentages are a clear demonstration of the principles we have been discussing, and, I would submit, fully justify the designation utrolocal which we have applied to the Iban system of marriage.

Let us next consider the changes in status which result from marrying out of one's natal *bilek* family. The *bilek* family, as we have established, is an autonomous corporate group, and furthermore, no man, woman or child can be a full member of more than one *bilek* family at any given time. Thus, when an individual marries into another *bilek* family this act means the relinquishment, for the time being, of all rights in his (or her) natal *bilek*, and the assumption of comparable rights in his (or her) affinal *bilek*. In other words, under Iban *adat*, marriage confers upon an affine full jural membership of his (or her) spouse's *bilek* family. These rights depend, of course, on the continuance of the marriage, and should divorce occur an out-marrying individual normally has no recourse but to return and resume membership of his (or her) natal *bilek*. [15] But when a stable marriage ensues, an affine comes to occupy a position of equal importance to his (or her) spouse, and to possess virtually equivalent rights within the *bilek* family. Indeed, it often happens, and especially in the case of men whose prowess has brought them social prestige, that an affine comes to play the dominant role in the managing of a *bilek* family's affairs.

THE PRINCIPLES OF FAMILY INHERITANCE

Having briefly described the composition of the *bilek* family and the way in which its members are recruited, we may turn to an examination of the principles governing inheritance, for these, under the Iban system of filiation, are of particular significance. Let us begin by considering the position of the natal and adopted members of the family. As has already been stressed, children become members by right of birth of either their father's or their mother's *bilek*—but it is always one or the other. Thus, the children of a man practising uxorilocal residence are the members of their mother's natal *bilek*, and of this local group alone. They have no rights of inheritance within their father's natal *bilek*, of which they are not resident members. Similarly, the children of a woman practising virilocal residence are members of their father's local group, and have no rights of inheritance in their mother's natal *bilek*. Adopted children are members of the *bilek* into which they have been adopted, and of this *bilek* only.

The general rule for both natural and adopted children is this: as long as they remain resident members of their own *bilek* family, sons and daughters possess full and equal rights of inheritance over the family estate. In other words, within a *bilek* siblings are parceners or co-heirs. There is thus recognition of neither primogeniture nor ultimogeniture, and no differentia-

31

tion between the sexes, nor between natural and adopted children. Instead, in matters of inheritance, siblings are equals. Their equivalence is well expressed in the phrase: '*menyadi tampong pala*' which the Iban use to describe them. These words, which have the literal meaning: 'siblings whose heads are joined', symbolize aptly the kind of relationship in which siblings stand. Another much-used phrase is: '*menyadi begulai pemai*' meaning 'siblings of common inheritance'.

However, should a man, upon marriage, permanently leave his natal *bilek*, he thereby relinquishes his parcenary rights over its estate, but acquires rights in the *bilek* into which he marries and settles down. The same applies to a woman who marries out of her *natal* apartment. An affine, then, possesses parcenary rights within the *bilek* of which he (or she) is a resident member [16].

We have now seen that the Iban *bilek* family is an autonomous, corporate group, all the resident members of which—natal, adopted and affinal—hold rights over its estate. As the Iban themselves put it: 'Whoever stands by the *bilek* (i.e. remains a resident member), he (or she) possesses the belongings, possesses the valuables' ('*Sapa tan ka bilek, iya empu utai, empu keresa*'). This was an utterance made at Rumah Nyala in 1950 during the formal discussion of the conditions which were to govern the adoption of an infant boy, and it was made by one of the men of the adopting family. It was a public pledge that as long as the adopted child elected to remain resident in their apartment he would possess identical rights of inheritance with the other members of the family. This fundamental principle of inheritance was reiterated many times during the course of the discussion—as it always is on such occasions. Finally, to clinch the matter, another of the adopting party put it even more trenchantly by abruptly asserting: 'Whoever stands by the *bilek*, even be he a Kayan, a Bukitan, a Punan, an Ukit, it matters not, he is the one who inherits the property' ('*Sapa tan ka bilek, Kayan, Pakatan, Punan, Ukit, enda iboh, iya empu keresa*'). Now, the Kayans, the Bukitans, the Punans and the Ukits are neighbouring tribes of the Rejang headwaters; all are alien, and the Kayans and Ukits, in particular, are the bitter traditional enemies of the Iban. When this is realized, the force of the utterance just quoted will be appreciated. It affirms that even an enemy and an alien, should he come to live in an Iban *bilek*, would, if he maintained his residence, hold equal rights of inheritance with the other members of the family. For Iban ears there could be no more emphatic avowal than this of the principle we have been considering.

As long then, as an individual remains resident in a *bilek*, he (or she) is one of the group in which ownership and inheritance are vested. Indeed, it is the family as a whole that holds common tenure of the conglomeration of property and other rights which constitute 'the *bilek*'. In other words, the Iban *bilek* family is a corporation aggregate. Thus, no one of its members holds the right to disinherit another. In life the members of a *bilek* are parceners, and even in death each member is entitled to his share of the family estate—that last inheritance which he carries with him to the after-world. An elder looks to his children and to his grandchildren within the *bilek* family to care for him in his old age, and to perform conscientiously the elaborate mortuary rites which must accompany his passing from this world to the next. To the Iban these mortuary rites and the furnishing of grave goods are matters of supreme importance, and all the senior surviving members of the *bilek* family are expected to join in their faithful performance. As the Iban themselves phrase it: 'As the mortuary rites are equally performed, so equally is the *bilek* estate inherited' ('*Enti blah ngelumbong, blah empu utai*').

THE POSITION OF 'PUN BILEK'

By the death of an elder a family is depleted of one of its members, but in matters of tenancy and tenure no drastic change ensues for those who are left behind; the *bilek* is theirs, as it was before, and as before they continue to occupy it and manage its affairs. Because of this system of continuing ownership in which an apartment and all its appurtenances pass without disjunction from one generation to the next, it is always possible—as far as the memories of the Iban will permit—to trace, generation by generation, the course of succession to each *bilek* estate. Now, while all the members of a *bilek* family, at any particular time, constitute what we have called a corporation aggregate, there is always one individual who can be singled out as the senior member by right of descent. In other words, while the *bilek* family, jurally viewed, is a corporate group, it is still recognized that there is one individual from whom the ownership and inheritance rights of all the other members of the family ultimately stem, irrespective of whether these members be natal, adopted or affinal. For such a person the Iban have a special term; he (or she) is called the *pun bilek*—literally, the root, or foundation of the *bilek*.

It is, of course, possible for a pair of siblings to occupy the position of *pun bilek*, but this is a decidedly rare event, and in the three long-houses of our sample only four *bilek* (or 3·7 %) fell into this category. [17] In most instances, all but one of a group of siblings marry out (each, as presently to be explained, taking a minor share of the family's heirloom property), so leaving only one of their number to become *pun bilek*. Furthermore, when it does happen that two adult siblings elect to remain in their natal *bilek*, partition almost invariably follows; that is, the *bilek* splits into two independent sections, with one sibling in each. So, there was not, in our sample, a single case of two or more married siblings being *pun bilek* in the same apartment, nor did I encounter such an arrangement anywhere else in Sarawak.

From these facts it will be clear that in collecting Iban genealogies it becomes a matter of critical importance to discover, at each generation level, which members of a sibling group married out, and which of them remained in the natal *bilek*, for only in this way is it possible to identify those individuals who lived and died as members of a particular *bilek* family. This vital information also leads to the tracing of *bilek* family partition, an important process presently to be discussed.

The *pun bilek* may be looked upon, then, as the nucleus of the *bilek* family. As the senior member by virtue of descent, he (or she) is a direct link with the past, the person through whom the property and other rights acquired by former members have been handed on to the present members of the family.

Let us first consider the contemporary *pun bilek* of the 107 *bilek* families of Rumah Nyala, Rumah Sibat and Rumah Tungku, all of whom could be identified with certainty. It will be necessary, however, to omit at this stage six *bilek* of a special kind known as *bilek berakup*. A *bilek berakup* is formed when two independent *bilek* families amalgamate to form a single unit[18], and in these cases there are always two distinct *pun bilek*—one from each of the constituent groups. The contemporary *pun bilek*, or senior members by right of descent, of the 101 remaining families are shown in Table 6.[19]

Table 6. *Contemporary 'pun bilek'*

Long-house	Males as *pun bilek*	Females as *pun bilek*	A pair of siblings as *pun bilek*
Rumah Nyala	11	12	1
Rumah Sibat	14	13	2
Rumah Tungku	20	27	1
Totals	45	52	4

Once again it will be noted that there is a fairly even balance between the sexes, females holding the position of *pun bilek* in 53·6 % of cases, and males in 46·4 %.

From genealogical investigation and study it is further possible to establish the identity of the former *pun bilek* of a family, and so construct what is, in effect, a kind of line of succession, though often it is only two or three generations in depth.[20] Such a line of succession includes all the previous holders of the position of *pun bilek*, and it is thus a line of all the descendants through whom the ownership rights of one particular *bilek* have been transmitted from one generation to the next. Reconstructing these lines of succession to the position of *pun bilek* is a laborious and painstaking task, but it is an imperative one for the understanding of Iban family structure. An examination of several hundred of these lines again shows that men tend to occupy the position of *pun bilek* just about as frequently as do women. Thus, although most of the lines which I collected were only three or four generations in length, the great majority of them (i.e. about 80%) included both males and females. In some instances, indeed, there was simple alternation: e.g. male, female, male, female. A few lines did contain four successive *pun bilek* of the same sex, but these were a distinct rarity: among the 107 *bilek* families of our sample I discovered only three instances of there having been four female *pun bilek* in succession, and only two instances of there having been four males. There is always a slight chance of this sort of succession occurring over three- or four-generation periods, but probability is against it. It can be predicted with assurance that were it possible to collect longer lines of succession, every one of them would be found to contain *pun bilek* of both sexes.

Our next Table summarizes the results of an analysis of all the different lines of succession which I was able to collect at Rumah Nyala, Rumah Sibat and Rumah Tungku.

Table 7. '*Pun bilek*'

Long-house	Male *pun bilek*	Female *pun bilek*
Rumah Nyala	25	43
Rumah Sibat	24	34
Rumah Tungku	55	59
Totals	104	136

The percentages in this instance (i.e. females 56·6%, and males 43·4%) are not quite so evenly balanced as in the previous tables[21], but they do confirm that utrolateral filiation is a fundamental feature of Iban social structure. In theory, either males or females may occupy the position of *pun bilek*, and in practice the position is occupied by men almost as often as it is by women.

INHERITANCE AND AFFINES

The position of the natal members of a *bilek* family in regard to inheritance is clear, for their prerogative depends on direct descent. Furthermore, as we have seen, an adopted child has conferred upon him exactly the same rights. But what of an affine whose membership dates only from the time of his (or her) marriage? By way of explanation let us consider the case of a man who marries out of his natal *bilek*. When such a man decides upon uxorilocal residence, and when, in the course of time, it becomes evident to all concerned that his marriage will be a lasting one, he receives from his natal *bilek* family a form of personal inheritance called *pemai*. The amount of *pemai* given to an out-marrying member varies considerably from case to case, for it depends largely on the degree to which the other senior members of the *bilek* family approve of the marriage that has been contracted. Cases do occur in which no *pemai* at all is given, while at the other extreme, planned marriages between members of wealthy families are often marked by a show of ostentation. Very commonly the *pemai* consists of a Chinese jar or a bronze gong, and of various smaller articles such as plates and bowls.

The giving of this *pemai* is an event of signal importance, for it constitutes the final fulfilling of a man's rights of inheritance as far as his natal *bilek* is concerned, and it further represents the formal termination of membership of his natal (or adoptive) *bilek* family. Henceforward, he is a full member of his wife's *bilek*. His *pemai*, or personal inheritance, becomes part of the estate of his wife's apartment, and all his energies are now devoted to the welfare of this new family; any valuables he may acquire (as, for example, on a *bejalai*, or journey) are the property—*meum et tuum*—of this group. In other words, when a man marries out of his own apartment and into another, he has conferred upon him full jural membership of a new corporate group, with all its attendant privileges and obligations. And the same, of course, applies to a woman.

Marriage then, is an event of great moment, and particularly for the spouse who is leaving his (or her) natal apartment. Out-marriage, as we have seen, involves a radical change in jural status. It is also an occasion of psychological stress for the out-marrying spouse, since she (or he) is, in a sense, abandoning her natal family. Thus, one informant remarked that out-marriage (*ngugi ka orang*) meant 'the casting away of one's father and mother' ('*itong udah buai apai indai*'). However, about 75% of Iban marriages are within the kindred[22], and so the stresses of out-marriage are often allayed by the fact that the out-marrying spouse is entering the household of fairly close kin.

The entry into a *bilek* of a new member by marriage is commonly marked by a minor but highly significant ceremony. Each Iban family possesses an heirloom plate (*pinggai asi*, lit. 'rice plate') which ranks amongst the foremost sacra of the *bilek*, and has especial symbolic importance. Usually, it hangs on one of the walls of the family apartment in a cane casing, together with augury sticks (*kayu burong*) which have been gathered, in the past, to consecrate major family undertakings. This *pinggai asi* is only used on ritual occasions, as, for example, during the rites which mark the first eating, by the assembled members of a household, of the new season's rice. When, on marriage, a new member joins a family she (or he) eats her first meal from their *pinggai asi*. When the meal is finished, the plate is at once turned upside down on the mat, and a prayer is uttered, beseeching that both spouses will live in health, prosperity and happiness. The over-turning of the plate is a magical act symbolizing the anchoring or fastening in the apartment of its new member. Thus, according to the Iban, the intention of the rite is to prevent the new member fretting about her (or his) natal *bilek* ('*ngambi iya badu betati ka bilek diri empu*').

If the marriage be a successful one, an affine is gradually absorbed, psychologically, into his (or her) new *bilek* family. As an example of this process let me cite the case of Gering, a young woman who, in 1941, left her natal long-house (in the Sungai Melinau) and married into a *bilek* family of Rumah Nyala (in the Sungai Sut). Gering relates that when she first came to Rumah Nyala she was very unhappy, and always pining for the *bilek* she had left behind; at night she often wept—especially when it thundered, for thunder can be a portent that one's close kin are suffering sickness or hurt. The fact that her natal long-house was two to three days' travel away—and arduous travel by way of rivers broken by hazardous rapids—made her situation even more desolate; but within a year of her marriage a son was born, and gradually Gering became resigned to her lot. By 1950, with two sons of her own, Gering had grown fully accustomed to life at Rumah Nyala. Indeed, when we took her back on a visit to her natal *bilek*, she said that it seemed, because of her long absence, to be 'like the *bilek* of strangers' ('*asai bilek orang laban lama*'), and she was more than happy to return to her husband's apartment. When we did arrive back at Rumah Nyala, Gering told us she felt really at home again: it was, she remarked 'as if her mother-in-law had become her mother'. Another informant observed that a son-in-law or a daughter-in-law (*menantu*) is thought of as being 'half a child' ('*itong se tengah anak*'); and I also heard it said that when a marriage occurs the parents-in-law 'adopt their *menantu* (son-in-law or daughter-in-law) as the twin of their own child' ('*ngambo menantu ka sapit anak*'). All of these statements are evidence of the deep significance of the change which marriage brings about in the status of an out-marrying individual.

IBAN MORTUARY CUSTOMS AND INHERITANCE

Further evidence of the status of affines in the Iban *bilek* family is to be had from an examination of Iban death customs and of the position of widows and widowers.

The Iban have an absolute and fervent belief in the immortality of the soul and in the existence of an after-world, which they call Sabayan. To this shadowy land go the souls of all the Iban dead—men, women and children. It is also an unshakeable Iban belief that all objects possess separable soul-counterparts, called *semengat*, and the Iban are utterly convinced that any article can be taken to the after-world in the form of its soul-counterpart. Sabayan, indeed, is looked upon as being an almost exact replica of this world, and it is the solemn duty of the living to equip the dead for their future existence. So it is that every dead person is furnished with burial property, or *baiya*. This burial property includes an exceedingly wide range of objects, from clothing, ornaments, weapons, tools, cooking utensils and rice seed, to precious beads, jars, gongs and fabrics. All of these things are either buried with the corpse, or left lying on the surface of the grave; and it is believed that all of them—in the shape of their soul-counterparts—are carried to the after-world by the soul of the dead man. He is helped in this task by a band of already departed kinsfolk (*antu Sabayan*), who come to offer their assistance, and to guide the soul on its ghostly journey to Sabayan.

The provision of adequate burial property is, to the Iban, a major responsibility. It is, in fact, a final inheritance: the equipping of a person with all the necessaries of social and economic life in the after-world.

Should a child die, it is the duty of the remaining members of the natal (or adoptive) *bilek* family to provide the burial property. What happens in the case of an adult? The answer to this question is clearly of importance to our analysis, for it will give an indication of the status of the affinal members in a *bilek* family. The rule is a simple one: a man's burial property is provided by the *bilek* family of which he was a resident member at the time of his death, irrespective of whether it was his natal apartment or the apartment of which he had become a member through marriage. This rule applies even though the marriage was a very recent one, and it refers equally to men and to women. In this all-important matter then, marriage is as much an arbiter of status and eligibility as are birth and adoption.

WIDOWS AND WIDOWERS

Finally, let us glance at the position of widows and widowers, and, in particular, let us examine the rights in respect of inheritance of those widows and widowers who are also affines, for these rights—as we shall see—are of especial significance. I would claim, indeed, that the examination of the position held by affinal widows and widowers is a crucial stage in the analysis of any corporate kin group.

In societies based on the principle of unilateral filiation affines commonly hold rights of a limited kind. In most patrilineal societies, for example, a woman even though practising virilocal residence, still retains membership and other rights within her natal lineage. The position of such a woman is made plain when she becomes a widow: in some patrilineal societies the levirate is practised, but in others a widow returns to resume residence as a member of her birth group. In Iban society, which is organized on other principles, the case is entirely different, and neither of these things happens. Among the Iban, a widow has every right to stay on as a member of her deceased husband's *bilek*, and, indeed, it is her acknowledged obligation to do so. True enough, in the event of death occurring in the very early stages of a marriage, a woman may perhaps elect—after the proper rites have been observed—to return to her natal apartment, but in all cases where the marriage

38

has been well established, and especially if there are children, there is an extremely strong tendency for wives to remain. And the same applies to a widower who has been practising uxorilocal marriage.

In the three long-houses Rumah Nyala, Rumah Sibat and Rumah Tungku there were, in all, fifty-two widows and widowers. Analysis shows that of these, twenty-six were widows and widowers living as members of their natal *bileks*, and twenty-six were widows or widowers in *bileks* of which they were members by right of marriage and prolonged local residence. Moreover, in the 107 *bilek* families of our sample, there was only one instance of a widow who had returned to her natal apartment, and she was a young woman of about twenty-two years, whose husband had died after she had been married for only four months.

These facts and figures are further evidence that when a man marries out of his natal *bilek* family and into that of his wife he acquires full jural membership of this affinal *bilek*. And the same thing happens when a woman marries out of the *bilek* into which she was born, and takes up virilocal residence. In summary then, we may say that in Iban society marriage involves a radical change in group membership for all out-marrying individuals, for within the *bilek* family marriage confers jural status just as do birth and adoption.

PARTITION

As the analysis so far has indicated, the Iban *bilek* family is a corporate group, holding property and other rights in absolute ownership. It has also been established that within the *bilek* family siblings have equivalent rights; in other words, they are parceners, or co-heirs. Implicit in this situation is the possibility that an adult sibling may claim his (or her) share of the family estate, secede from the ancestral *bilek*, and set up a separate domestic unit. This is exactly what does happen; and, indeed, it is a common occurrence in Iban society. [23]

The process is, I think, best described as *partition*, for what happens is the division of a *bilek* into two distinct parts, each part becoming an autonomous unit in its own right. The Iban term describing this event is *kadiri*, which means 'to become separate'. The fundamental feature of the process is that each part, after partition has occurred, is a fully independent entity, and not merely a constituent segment of some wider corporate group. The partition of *bilek* families as it occurs in Iban society is thus a distinctly different process from segmentation as it occurs in societies based on unilineal principles. In these societies—whether patrilineal or matrilineal—segments are always, in some degree, component parts of a more inclusive lineage or clan, and within the society as a whole the status of each segment is determined by its relative position within this hierarchical system. [24] In Iban society, on the other hand, although *bilek* families are always linked by cognatic ties, they are fully autonomous units both socially and jurally, and of independent and equal status. The distinction may be summed up by saying that whereas the segments of a lineage are a system of aliquot parts, Iban *bilek* families—resulting from partition—are a series of discrete units.

Let us now examine the process of partition more closely. As we have already noted, the Iban *bilek* family is a corporation aggregate, all the *bilek* property and other rights being held in common by all members of the family. This does not mean, of course, that there is no concept of personal property. A man's clothes are his own, as are his various accoutrements and most of the weapons he uses; and in the same way, a woman has her own garments and jewellery. But all the really valuable possessions (*peseka*) of the *bilek*, made up of bronze gongs and cannons, Chinese jars, plates and bowls, woven fabrics, beads and ceremonial attire, trophy heads, charms and other sacra, plantations of fruit trees and tracts of rice land, are held in common family ownership. For any particular *bilek*, most of this property will have been acquired by past generations of the family, but the present members will also have contributed their share. All the members of a family, as we have seen, work together to grow the rice and other foods they require, for in this, as in all economic pursuits, they co-operate to form a single producing and consuming unit. So, whenever the rice crop is an abundant one, part of the surplus is always used to purchase property for the *bilek*, and, similarly, the men of the family, when they undertake their expeditions (*bejalai*)—whether inland to gather jungle produce, or to the coast to work for wages—are expected to return home with some article of value to add to the common inheritance.

This system of common ownership, production and consumption by the *bilek* family works satisfactorily enough as long as the group remains restricted in numbers. In the case of small families, such as those consisting of a man, his wife and their children, it is, indeed, an ideal arrangement, for there is a complete concurrence of interests. But later in the history of such a household stresses very frequently develop. In most families one at least of the children marries out, and so attains membership of some other apartment; but it often happens that two or more of the other sons and daughters elect to remain as members of their natal *bilek*. Should two of these siblings become married while still residing in their natal *bilek*, processes are set in train which almost inevitably end in partition.

Within the *bilek* family siblings are equals, owning the same rights and obligations, and as such they are joined by strong bonds of solidarity. But when, in the course of time, these siblings marry and children are born, this results in the intrusion of new and rival loyalties. The *bilek* family is no longer a simple group, for it now contains within its boundaries two different elementary families, and when two elementary families emerge within the confines of the same apartment there is a very strong tendency for their interests to diverge.

This divergence is prompted by many different factors. Between families sharing the same *ménage* and the same cramped quarters, disagreements and misunderstandings readily arise. There are, for example, numerous occasions, for partiality and favouritism, and these easily lead to heart-burning and resentment. A man returning from a journey to the coast brings back more and much better gifts for his own wife and children than he does for his sister and her children, and so breaks the rule that within the *bilek* there should be equal sharing. Or there arises the more serious complaint that one couple are not participating as they should in the arduous work of rice farming, on which the very subsistence of the *bilek* depends. A wife, on some pretext or other, shirks part of the back-breaking task of weeding, and her husband's sister broods over it as she toils in the heat of the sun. A younger brother-in-law is always gadding off on journeys and neglecting the sterner and duller work of farming. Such defections from corporate obligations may take many forms, for among the Iban personal inclination is given unusually free rein, but almost always they refer in some way to unequal participation in work and the unequal sharing of its fruits, and these we may single out as the basic sources of dissatisfaction.[25]

Very often partition is preceded by disagreements which culminate in quarrelling. The beginnings are usually small, and their accretion gradual, but aggravation follows aggravation until at last the storm breaks. One of the wives of a *bilek* finds her position intolerable; she whispers her complaints to others in the long-house, and before long her barbed words of condemnation percolate back to the person against whom they were directed. In retaliation the process is repeated, until at last there is quarrelling and an open breach in the family. According to the Iban themselves, resentment (*pedis ati*) at the words and behaviour of some other member of the *bilek* is the circumstance which most often precipitates partition. My own observations fully bore out this conclusion that disagreements and discord are closely associated with the break-up of *bilek* families, but it is important to note that they are almost always the outcome of stresses implicit in the existence of two elementary families in the same household. Furthermore, when quarrelling does occur between the elementary families of a *bilek* it is usual to find that one or both of the two affinal members are involved. This leads us to the heart of the matter. A group of unmarried siblings have a united interest in the welfare of their natal *bilek*, and it is only by marriage that the opportunity to set up separate apartments is created. When siblings who are members of the same *bilek* do marry, their unity is at once threatened by the rival loyalty which they now have towards their spouses, and this incipient cleavage, which is accentuated by the arrival of children and the setting up of families, almost always ends in complete separation. In other words, when they exist within the same *bilek*, the sibling tie and the conjugal tie are opposed forces—the one centripetal, or tending to hold the *bilek* together, and the other centrifugal or tending to split it into separate parts. In the great majority of cases, it is the conjugal tie which proves the stronger, and eventually causes the *bilek* to sub-divide.

This is borne out by an analysis of the composition of *bilek* families at the time when partition occurs. In the three long-houses of our sample there were thirty-six *bileks* which had sub-divided, and approximately 80 % of these were *bileks* which contained two married siblings (and their spouses) at the time when partition took place. In each case one of the couples (accompanied by their children, where these existed) broke away to set up an apartment of their own. This percentage is evidence which supports our conclusion that divergence or conflict of interest between the families of siblings is a preponderating factor in the process of *bilek* partition.

But what of families with no recent record of partition? Does it ever happen that married siblings do manage to achieve an harmonious and enduring partnership as members of the same *bilek*? My observations, both in the Third and Second Divisions of Sarawak, suggest that it is very rare for such a thing to happen. For more than two married siblings to occupy the same *bilek* is an entirely unheard-of event; and in the three Baleh long-houses of our sample there were only eight out of a total of 107 *bileks* in which a pair of married siblings were living as members of the same household. This is a small enough proportion, but far from all of these *bileks* could be characterized as stable groups. In two instances partition was actually in the course of being arranged when I left the Baleh region in 1951, and, in addition, there were two marginal cases in which, following temporary stability, there were discernible signs that partition was impending. In three of the other *bileks* one of the marriages was very recent and it was too early to descry any developments one way or the other. The remaining case was the only really stable and long-standing sibling partnership in the three communities, and it was an unusual one in which two sisters had taken as their husbands two brothers from a neighbouring long-house.[26]

For a pair of married siblings to be members of the same *bilek* family is, then, a rare event, occurring in not more than about 5 % of all *bileks*. Furthermore, a study of the eight examples we have just discussed and of a series of other recent cases of partition, strongly suggests that even when a pair of married siblings do achieve an amicable partnership, it seldom lasts for more than about ten years. As soon as the two couples have established thriving families of their own, the desire for independence is too strong to be resisted, and the families separate, each to seek its individual fortune. The positive advantages of independence are many. Having a *bilek* of their own gives a man and his wife the opportunity to live and work without interference, and in the knowledge that they will not have to share the fruits of their labours with others. To the Iban, who are nothing if not calculating and ambitious individualists, this is an immense attraction. We may say then, that with singularly few exceptions the emergence of two elementary families within the same *bilek* eventually leads to partition. Indeed, the process is so widely prevalent, and so regular, that it may be cited as a sociological principle, and singled out as one of the fundamental features of Iban social structure.

THE PROCESS OF PARTITION

I have described partition as an event which occurs with remarkable regularity in certain social situations, but this is not to suggest that it is, in any sense, an automatic process, like, for example, the fission of cells. The partition of a *bilek* only occurs when a certain section of its members decide for definite reasons to break away and set up a separate apartment of their own. Acts of choice and decision are always involved, even though they are always within the narrow range of alternatives permitted by the structure of Iban society. This leads us to the very important point that when a *bilek* family divides into two groups one of them is always the instigating group—the group, that is, whose actions precipitate the process of partition, and whose insistence brings it to fulfilment. This instigating group is always the one which breaks away physically to build, and then to occupy, a new residential apartment of the long-house. Again, almost without exception, its members are younger than the oldest individual of the group which is left in possession of the ancestral *bilek* of the family.

In discussing partition it will be convenient, therefore, to refer to the instigating and seceding group as the junior section of the family, and to the passive and stationary group as the senior section.

A further point of importance is that the junior or seceding section usually has fewer members than the senior section. Thus analysis shows that, on the average, a *bilek* family contains about eight or nine members at the time when partition occurs, with the senior section having five or six, and the junior section three or four members. We may say then, that the predominant pattern of *bilek* partition is for a junior and minor group to secede from a senior and major group.

As its limited size suggests, the seceding section is generally a very simple group, consisting—in the great mass of cases—of a married couple and their children. In short, partition is predominantly concerned with small and newly founded families that decide to break away, to build a home of their own, and to manage their own affairs.

This brings us to another fundamental feature of the Iban family system. It will be obvious that partition is out of the question if a family has only one child, for this individual is then the sole heir. In other words, partition only occurs when a *bilek* family contains two or more siblings. Furthermore, without exception, a brother or sister of the seceding sibling is always left behind in the ancestral *bilek*.[27] This permits us to formulate the general rule that partition always involves the break-up of a sibling group. Here, I would submit, we have a principle of cardinal importance, for it defines in precise terms the essential character of *bilek* family partition as it exists among the Iban.

Summarily then, we may say that partition consists of the secession of a son (or daughter), with spouse and children, from his (or her) natal *bilek*, this natal *bilek* being left in the possession of his (or her) parents and their remaining children and grandchildren.

THE DIVISION OF THE FAMILY ESTATE

A brief word may now be said concerning the way in which the partition of a *bilek* estate is achieved. Under Iban *adat*, the *bilek* is, in general, a partible estate. Thus, as we have seen, should a sibling and spouse elect to part company with the other members of the family, it is recognized that they have a lawful and undeniable claim to a proportionate share of the conglomeration of property and other rights which make up the inheritable possessions of the *bilek*. But there are certain exceptions of the greatest consequence, for two ritual objects, in particular, are strictly non-partible. Both are associated with the growing of rice.

In Iban eyes, rice (*padi*) is by far the most precious thing which they possess: it is the main source from which wealth flows, and upon its successful cultivation all well-being depends. To the Iban, however, the cultivation of rice is not so much a problem in agricultural method as a problem in ritual knowledge and skill. Their *padi*, so the Iban believe, is a spirit, and a farmer's success depends pre-eminently on his ability to order his dealings with the *padi* spirits in such a way as to win their approval, and so to attract to himself the bountiful crops that all men desire. To this end, the Iban have, through the centuries, devised a series of most elaborate rites. Almost all of these rites are focused upon a strain of sacred rice known as *padi pun*. Each year a tiny patch of this sacred rice is sown in the centre of the farm clearing, and there is performed the intricate sequence of magico-religious rituals upon which rests the fertility of all the *padi* that has been planted. Here, however, we are concerned only with the fact that every *bilek* family has its own particular variety of sacred rice. Unlike ordinary kinds of rice, *padi pun* is never sold or given away, for this would be to dissipate its magical efficacy acquired during the countless rituals carried out by past generations. In addition to its *padi pun*, a *bilek* family also possesses three or four subsidiary strains of sacred rice. These are termed *sangking*, and each year they are sown in small plots immediately surrounding the *padi pun* itself. Although all rituals are focused primarily on the *padi pun*, the several *sangking* also fall within their ambit. As one Iban put it, it is rather as though the *padi pun* were the eldest of a band of brothers.

It is one of the axioms of Iban *adat* that the *padi pun* of a *bilek* is non-partible. What then is the solution when a family sub-divides into two separate households? Briefly it is this: the senior section retains possession of the *padi pun*, while the seceding section is presented with one of the *sangking*, which is then elevated to become its *padi pun*. Here, clearly, we have a criterion of crucial importance for the study of the process of *bilek* family formation in Iban society. The senior section of a family is always definable by the fact that its *padi pun* was inherited as *padi pun*; while the *padi pun* of a seceding section is always inherited as *sangking*. By studying the inheritance of *padi pun* and *sangking*, therefore, it is possible to establish the main line of a family, and the various offshoots from it which have been brought about by partition.

A second non-partible object is the *batu pemanggol*, or ritual whetstone, which is the centre-piece of the rites that initiate the yearly farming cycle. Each *bilek* family possesses one of these stones which is cherished as a magical charm of most vital importance. A few Iban families, indeed, still have whetstones upon which human victims—captives taken in war—were once sacrificed. Such stones are called *batu jaum*, and are immeasurably valuable in Iban estimation. To divide a *batu pemanggol* would be to destroy it, and so, when partition takes place, it is always retained in the ancestral *bilek*. The seceding section, seeking an auspicious occasion, gathers a suitable-looking stone from the river bed. With a great show of solemnity, the new stone is touched on the old and then consecrated; tutelary spirits are invoked and offerings made, and finally a pig or cock is sacrificed and the blood allowed to run on the stone's surface. This stone then becomes the *batu pemanggol* of the seceding section.

When partition occurs then, the senior section of the family always retains the ancestral sacred rice and ritual whetstone. It may also happen that a *bilek* possesses some other unique magical or ritual object and, if this be the case, this too is retained by the senior section. With these exceptions, however, all the other property of the *bilek* is partible, and its apportionment is in accord with the relative size and the composition of the two sections resulting from the partition, following the general rule that siblings are parceners.

More often than not the apportionment of the *bilek* property is carried out by the siblings and others concerned in private conference. But cases do occasionally happen in which feelings run so high that agreement cannot be reached, and in this event the *tuai rumah* and other elders of the long-house are called in to act as assessors and adjudicators. They meet in the apartment of the family concerned, where all the non-personal, inheritable property has been heaped up in the centre of the room. All the members of the family are present and the composition of the two sections seeking partition is well known to all taking part. After a brief interchange of views the value of the various items of the assembled property is formally assessed and they are then all allotted in the proper proportions to the two sections. In addition to the adjudicating elders there are always a number of other outside witnesses and so the partition becomes a final and binding settlement. The occasion concludes by one of the elders waving a cock, in blessing, over the divided sections of the family, and uttering a prayer that henceforward they will live in concord and their affairs prosper.

Finally, there is one further aspect of the process of *bilek* partition that deserves mention. It has been shown that the *pun bilek* of a family—the senior member by right of descent—may be either a man or a woman, and that, in fact, males and females occupy the position of *pun bilek* to an approximately equal extent. It has also been remarked that when partition takes place the seceding section always contains a sibling. This individual, it will be clear, is the *pun bilek* of the new apartment. Now, in Iban society, siblings are equals and co-heirs, and again, in matters of tenancy and tenure, there is no differentiation of rights in terms of sex. From these principles one would infer that when partition occurs there is an equal likelihood of a daughter seceding from her ancestral *bilek* as there is of a son seceding. This inference is well borne out by the facts. In the three long-houses, Rumah Nyala, Rumah Sibat and Rumah Tungku, there were thirty-six cases of partition, all of which had occurred during the lifetime of one of the members of the *bileks* concerned. Table 8 presents an analysis of the status of the *pun bilek* of the seceding sections in these thirty-six cases of partition.

Table 8. '*Pun bilek*' of seceding sections in '*bilek*'
family partition

Long-house	Male *pun bilek*	Female *pun bilek*	Two brothers as *pun bilek*	Brother and sister as *pun bilek*
Rumah Nyala	4	1	–	–
Rumah Sibat	6	7	1	1
Rumah Tungku	7	9	–	–
Totals	17	17	1	1

It will be seen that there were two instances in which the seceding section contained a pair of siblings: a brother and sister in one instance, and a pair of brothers in the other. In thirty-four cases, however, the seceding section contained only one sibling. It is noteworthy that of these seventeen were daughters who had seceded from their ancestral *bileks* and seventeen were sons. Here again we are confronted with that equal balancing between the sexes which is such a salient feature of the Iban family system.

CONCLUSION

The purpose of this essay has been mainly descriptive: the presentation in succinct terms of the principal features of what is, I believe, a theoretically significant type of family structure. Radcliffe-Brown and others have frequently pointed to the special interest of the cognatic family and kinship systems found in the societies of Malaysia, but as yet our understanding of them is very limited. To the best of my knowledge this is the first time that a family system of the Iban type has been described, but there are good grounds for supposing that closely similar systems are to be found elsewhere in Borneo as well as in other parts of Malaysia.

Our analysis has directed particular attention to the principle of utrolateral filiation on which the Iban family system rests. That is, in Iban society, a child is always a member of either its father's or its mother's natal *bilek*, depending on whether its parents practice virilocal or uxorilocal marriage; it is never a member of both their *bileks*, but always of one or the other. Furthermore, filiation to the paternal *bilek* and filiation to the maternal *bilek* occur with very nearly equal incidence. It has also been stressed that an essential feature of the Iban system is the existence of a clearly defined local entity—the *bilek* estate—to which individuals are filiated or attached. In other words, membership of the Iban *bilek* family is based partly on descent and partly on local residence, and it is these two principles working together which produce what we have called a system of utrolateral filiation. This fact that the *bilek* is invariably a single local unit is intrinsic to Iban family organization. Indeed, one might put forward the view that it is only by the recognition of some criterion of local residence that corporate kin groups can be formed in societies based on cognatic principles.

Of the complex inter-relationships which link the *bilek* families of a long-house community little has been said: this is an aspect of Iban social organization which must be discussed on another occasion. In this essay we have been concerned solely with the *bilek* family. That the *bilek* family merits this concern there can be small doubt, for, as we have seen, it is the basic corporate kin group of Iban society. In the words of Temenggong Jugah: 'Among us Iban each *bilek* is like a sovereign country.'

47

J. D. FREEMAN

A NOTE ON PARTITION AND OUT-MARRIAGE AND THE SIZE OF THE SIBLING GROUP

A special problem with which one has to deal in attempting to explain the working of the Iban family system is the differential incidence of out-marriage and partition.

An obvious way of coping with this question is to examine a series of different sibling groups and to determine, for each of them, the relative incidence of out-marriage, adoption out of the *bilek*, and *bilek* partition.

One necessary condition for a survey of this kind is that all the sibling groups considered should have reached a stage at which all of the processes to be examined had reached a state of completion.

Accordingly, I extracted from my collection of genealogies for R. Nyala, R. Sibat and R. Tungku, all the available cases of this kind. This gave me ninety-eight sibling groups in all—ranging in size from one to nine members.

For all of these ninety-eight groups I noted the instances of out-marriage, adoption out, and partition—where they occurred—and then tabulated the results. The results for out-marriage and partition are tabulated in the diagram opposite.

Along the horizontal axis of the graph the ninety-eight sibling groups of the sample are arranged in order of size from one to nine; and along the vertical axis frequencies are shown as percentages, cases of out-marriage, as they occurred, as a percentage of all possible cases; cases of partition, as they occurred, as a percentage of the total number of cases of partition which might have occurred.

The diagram can be summarized verbally, as follows:

Size of sibling group	ref.: out-marriage and partition
1	Partition never occurs; out-marriage is exceedingly rare (5 % of cases); (i.e. sole heir always remains in natal *bilek*, except in highly rare and unusual circumstances).
2	Out-marriage and partition *about equal* (e.g. 47 % : 44 %).
3	Out-marriage *slightly more common* than partition (e.g. 53 % : 37 %).
4	Out-marriage *about twice as common* as partition (e.g. 66 % : 29 %).
5	Out-marriage remains *markedly* more common than partition (e.g. about twice as common).

Let us now glance at the phenomenon of out-marriage.

OUT-MARRIAGE

We can, I think, on the evidence from our sample of ninety-eight sibling groups, make a generalization something of this kind:

The incidence of marriage out of natal *bilek* families (i.e. into other *bilek* families) exhibits a slight tendency to progressive increase as the size of sibling groups (in *bilek* families) progressively increases.

(E.g. from an average incidence of 48% in the case of sibling groups of two members to an average incidence of 60% in the cases of sibling groups of five and over.)

POSSIBLE EXPLANATIONS OF THIS TENDENCY

(1) As a sibling group increases in numbers the potential share of any one individual of the *bilek* estate decreases. (E.g. sole heir inherits whole of estate, two children inherit half each, three one-third each, and so on.) This means that as a

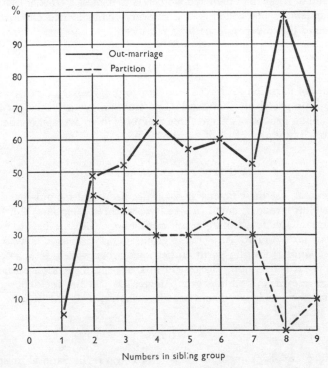

sibling group increases in size it becomes increasingly less 'worth while' for any member of the group to remain in his natal *bilek*, with the intention of claiming his share of the *bilek* estate. In other words, it is more 'worth while' (i.e. in his material, social and other interests) for any member of a large sibling group to marry out of his natal *bilek* and into another with only one or two members in its sibling group. He thus tends to inherit more property; and to acquire, as a result of this, greater social and ritual standing and influence.

(*Note*. To test this notion I made a separate analysis of all cases of males who had married into *bilek* families in which the potential *pun bilek* was an only daughter. There were nine such cases. It is, I think, significant that the average size of the sibling groups of these nine males was 6·3 members, whereas the average for the sample as a whole was 3·6.)

(2) The male members of large sibling groups are presented with greater opportunities for going on *bejalai* because their services in farming are not so vitally

required. This presents them with greater opportunities for meeting nubile females and settling down in other areas. The inducement for such males to return to a large *bilek* family is not so great.

(3) All Iban apartments are of about the same size. As a large family grows up living in this confined space becomes increasingly uncongenial. For members of large families out-marriage is the easiest avenue of escape. (Partition is a much more difficult operation, for other members of the sibling group may offer opposition, etc.)

(4) The aim of most Iban men and women is to possess a *bilek* of their own. This confers the independence which is dear to every Iban's heart. Out-marriage is an easier avenue to this independence than partition.

PARTITION

The incidence of partition exhibits a tendency to progressive decrease as the size of sibling groups progressively increases. (E.g. from an average incidence of 44% in the case of sibling groups of two to three members to an average incidence of 21% in the case of sibling groups of five and over.)

SUGGESTED EXPLANATIONS

These, in general, are the converse of what has been said for out-marriage.

When a sibling group is small in size (two to three members) the share of the family estate available to a sibling is sufficiently large (i.e. one-half to one-third) to provide strong inducement. As a sibling group increases in size, however, the share available to a sibling desiring partition becomes progressively less, so offering less inducement towards partition. Because of this, out-marriage offers stronger inducements as the size of the sibling group increases. So the incidence of partition decreases and the incidence of out-marriage increases as the size of the sibling group increases.

NOTES

[1] The Iban are also sometimes called Sea Dayaks. In Sarawak it so happened that the first Iban with whom the British came into contact (in the early 1840's) were certain groups of warriors, who, in league with Malays, had become addicted to coastal piracy. Understandably enough they were given the name of Sea Dayaks. However, from an ecological point of view the term Sea Dayak is inaccurate and misleading: the vast majority of the Iban have always been a hill people, living many miles from the coast, and their economy is essentially an agricultural one. The name Iban (which was introduced to ethnographical literature by Haddon in 1901) has now achieved general acceptance (Haddon 1901: 325).

[2] For an account of the Iban migrations into the Baleh region see Freeman 1955: 11 ff.

[3] I would like to express my most sincere thanks to the Colonial Social Science Research Council under whose auspices my field research was carried out.

[4] *Kami* is the personal pronoun: we, plural (excluding the person or persons addressed).

[5] Temenggong Jugah, of Sungai Merirai, Baleh region. Temenggong Jugah was one of the Colony of Sarawak's representatives at the Coronation of Her Majesty

Queen Elizabeth II. I was fortunate in that he was able to spend some time with me in Cambridge, where we renewed our friendship and discussed together the results of my analysis of Iban society.

[6] *Rumah* is the Iban word for a long-house; to this is added the name of the current *tuai rumah*, or headman of the community, e.g. Nyala.

[7] The average for Pengulu Jenggut's district (lower Batang Baleh and Sungai Sut) was 5·78 persons per *bilek*; while that for Pengulu Grinang's district (upper Batang Baleh and Sungai Gat) was also 5·75. These figures, which are for 1948, were obtained from official records at Kapit fort.

[8] It is, of course, possible for a *bilek* to become extinct because of an epidemic or some other natural catastrophe, but this—despite the hazardous environment to which the Iban are exposed—is an exceedingly rare happening.

[9] By filiation I mean to denote the system whereby an individual establishes membership of a structurally continuing group by virtue of birth (or adoption), and with reference to one of his (or her) parents (cf. *Oxford English Dictionary*, 'filiation, the fact of being the child of a specified parent').

[10] From the Latin, *uter*, either of two, one or the other, one of two.

[11] The *nusop ayu* ritual, the main design of which is the 'transplanting' of the adopted child's *ayu*, or 'soul' in the same clump as the *ayu* of the members of his adoptive *bilek* family.

[12] Based on investigation of the reproductive histories of thirty-four women of Rumah Nyala; inquiries conducted at other long-houses of the Baleh region showed closely comparable results. For conducting these, as many other inquiries, I am deeply indebted to my wife.

[13] Based on interviews with seventy-seven women (all of whom had passed menopause) of Rumah Nyala, Rumah Sibat and Rumah Tungku.

[14] It is, in fact, rare in Iban society for first-cousins to be members of the same *bilek* family. Cases do occur of young children who are first-cousins occupying the same *bilek*, but by the time they have reached puberty, partition has almost always taken place. In only one of the 107 *bileks* of our sample did the possibility of first-cousin intra-*bilek* incest exist; moreover first-cousins of this kind have grown up, in the same household, to look upon one another as siblings, and between them sexual relations or marriage would be unthinkable.

[15] Cases do very occasionally occur in which a natal spouse will, following divorce (usually instigated by adultery), move to another apartment; in such instances the deserted affinal spouse will usually stay on in the *bilek* of which he (or she) is a member by right of marriage. This and other happenings associated with divorce are of especial interest, but in a summary essay of this kind it is not possible to give them the detailed discussion they deserve.

[16] The nature of an affine's rights depend, as might be expected, on duration of residence. In the event of early divorce they are, of course, abrogated, but should a man die in his wife's *bilek*, he is treated in the provision of grave goods and the like just as though he were a natal member. This point will be taken up when we come to discuss the position of widows and widowers.

[17] In three of these instances only one of the siblings was married, while the other was single; and the fourth case was that of two sisters both of whom were divorcees.

[18] Amalgamation is a rare event, for it is only resorted to when one or both of the two *bileks* concerned are in such a straitened state as to make independent survival either difficult or impossible. The most common cause is the reduction of the personnel of a *bilek* by death.

[19] In all cases of affinal widows or widowers and their children succeeding, the *bilek* has been reckoned as 'belonging' to the dead spouse—the last determinable *pun bilek*.

[20] The Iban of the Baleh region make no attempt to preserve lengthy genealogies and the longest line of succession that I collected was one of five generations, including the *pun bilek* who was still living. The Iban, in their bilateral society, are much more interested in the spread or scatter of relationships, where—in the absence of exact genealogical knowledge—they are guided by their classificatory system of kinship.

[21] That the proportions do not, in practice, work out as equally as one would predict from theoretical premises is significant, for it indicates that males marry out of their natal *bileks* slightly more often than do females. This tendency—running counter to complete utrolaterality—is probably to be accounted for by the fact that whereas Iban men regularly travel far away from their homes and so visit many other long-houses, where marriages are likely to be contracted, the womenfolk undertake such journeys very rarely indeed.

[22] I am using kindred in the same sense as W. H. R. Rivers: 'a group consisting of persons related to one another, other than by marriage, through both father and mother' (Rivers 1924: 16).

[23] For example, thirty-six of the 107 *bilek* families of our sample had come into being by process of partition during the lifetime of one of their living members.

[24] As, for example, among the Tallensi: '...every minimal lineage is a segment of a more inclusive lineage defined by reference to a common grandfather, and this, in turn, is a segment of a still wider lineage defined by reference to a common great-grandfather; and so on until the limit is reached—the maximal lineage, defined by reference to the remotest agnatic ancestor of the group' (Fortes 1945: 31).

[25] So Temenggong Jugah (of Sungai Merirai), a most intelligent Iban leader, gives as the main sources of *bilek* family partition: '*ari begarih*', and '*ari enggai besangkong*'. '*Ari begarih*' means 'from claiming more than one's fair share, from dividing something unequally'; while '*ari enggai besangkong*' means 'from refusal to get anything for a person whilst getting it for oneself', or, 'from refusal to co-operate on a basis of reciprocity' (Howell and Bailey 1900: 47, 148).

[26] In the two long-houses—Gansurai (nineteen doors), of Sungai Layar, and Plandok (thirteen doors), of Sungai Paku—which I studied in the Saribas district of the Second Division of Sarawak, there was not a single instance of married siblings occupying the same *bilek*.

[27] When the family is a large one as many as four or five siblings may be left behind in the ancestral *bilek*, and it sometimes happens that, after a lapse of years, another sibling marries and partition takes place a second time. It should also be noted that the senior section usually (i.e. in about 90% of cases) contains one or both of the parents of the seceding son or daughter. This means that when *bileks* divide they almost always divide into groups which are unequal both in numbers and in generation seniority.

REFERENCES CITED

Baring-Gould, S. and Bampfylde, C. A. 1909, *A History of Sarawak*, London.

Fortes, M. 1945, *The Dynamics of Clanship among the Tallensi*, Oxford.

Freeman, J. D. 1955, *Iban Agriculture: A Report on the Shifting Cultivation of Hill Rice by the Iban of Sarawak*, H.M.S.O. London.

Haddon, A. C. 1901, *Head-Hunters: Black, White and Brown*, London.

Haddon, A. C. and Start, L. E. 1936. *Iban or Sea Dayak Fabrics*, Cambridge.

Howell, W. and Bailey, D. J. S. 1900, *A Sea Dayak Dictionary*, Singapore.

Murdock, G. P. 1949, *Social Structure*, New York.

Rivers, W. H. R. 1924, *Social Organization*, London.

THE FISSION OF DOMESTIC GROUPS
AMONG THE LODAGABA

By JACK GOODY

INTRODUCTION

In this paper I want to discuss the problem of growth and fission of domestic groups among the LoDagaba of the Northern Territories of the Gold Coast. The debt to Fortes' study of the domestic organization of the Tallensi is immediately obvious to anyone acquainted with this work. This partly arises from the ethnographic proximity of the LoDagaba and the Tallensi. Both live in the orchard bush country within the Niger bend, being situated about 100 miles apart in the vicinity of the 11th parallel. Both speak languages of the Mossi (or Mole-Dagbane) group of the Gur family. Their productive systems, based upon the hoe cultivation of millet and guinea corn, are very similar and they share many of the same cultural practices.

But the debt does not merely result from the analysis of similar ethnographic material. It is also a matter of the general approach. Fortes' study of the domestic organization of the Tallensi in *The Web of Kinship* was based, in addition to descriptive records, upon a sociological census of a sample of homesteads. Such a survey gives statements essentially synchronic in nature, referring to the point in time at which the census was taken. Examples of these are: 'the characteristic form of the joint family of the Tallensi is the agnatic joint family' (Fortes 1949(a): 64) and 'the modal number of wives is one' (1949(a): 66). The thoroughness with which this survey was carried out and the way in which domestic groups were examined within the context of more inclusive units represented a significant advance in social anthropology. However, Fortes' contribution was not limited to the detailed synchronic analysis of the data, significant as this was. Whereas previous writers had tended to treat the spread in the composition of domestic groups as deviations from a modal or from an ideal type, Fortes pointed out that 'other forms of domestic group appear as phases in the growth cycle of a joint family' (1949(a): 64). His approach is succinctly summarized in the following passage:

The domestic group grows, changes, and dissolves with the growth cycle of (the effective minimal) lineage, and a particular elementary family is only an episode in this cycle. The structure of the Tale family cannot be divorced from its existence in time. We have to examine it as a process. At any given time

53

we find domestic families at every stage of development in a Tale community (1949(*a*): 63).

Like many of the statements of social science, once formulated they may seem apparent enough, merely the application of 'common sense'. One wonders why 'common sense' nevertheless eludes so many. The proper perspective can only be gained by the introduction of the time element, by a comparison with the work of earlier anthropologists. Such a comparison was made implicitly by Fortes himself in the fieldwork he subsequently undertook on the Ashanti. The complexities of Ashanti domestic organization were such that a greater emphasis had to be placed upon numerical information. By means of this Fortes corrected certain basic assumptions of earlier writers.

The Ashanti were in many ways extremely well documented, largely due to the work of Rattray. But despite a long sojourn in the country and a thorough knowledge of the language, Rattray appears to have thought that marriage among the Ashanti was essentially virilocal. He acknowledges in several places that there are dwelling groups which are not so organized, but he regards these as deviations from a modal type. Rattray was probably misled in two ways. First, he seems to have accepted the ideal type as the modal type; he falls into a confusion between the actor's and observer's points of view. Secondly, he seems to accept the rigid dichotomy between virilocal and uxorilocal marriage; it had to be either one or the other.

That Rattray accepted the Ashanti version of their marriage, both in terms of preferential spouses and location, can be seen from his account of the course of family development.

The head of an Ashanti family is, as I have shown, the maternal uncle. Under his roof will be found his sons, their wives and children, and his unmarried daughters. His nephews and unmarried nieces live, while their father is alive, under his roof. As marriage is patrilocal, as soon as the nieces are grown up and married they go to the house of their husband's father. If, then, they marry their uncle's sons, it will be to his house that they will go. The nephews will remain in their father's house and will bring their brides there. On the death of their father they will probably go, with their wives and families, to their uncle's house, and so if they married their uncle's daughters the women return to the house in which they were born and brought up. If, on the other hand, the nieces do not marry their uncle's sons or the nephews his daughters, on marriage these women go away, possibly to some distant village, and the family tie is considerably weakened, for there can be little doubt that the question of residence in the uncle's house entails considerably increased control. (Rattray 1927: 326.)

The analysis of some of the results of the Ashanti Social Survey published in 'Time and Social Structure' (Fortes 1949(*b*)) showed that though it is the ideal of husbands to establish their own households at marriage and to have their wives join them there, this picture of the situation fails to reckon with the strength of the sibling bond. In Agogo, for example, the observed norm is against a wife living with her husband. Of the cases which do occur, approximately half are accounted for by cross-cousin marriage, but this nevertheless forms a very low percentage of the total marriages.

Rattray too conducted a census of marriages, but the results were never published. His scattered remarks show that he regarded non-virilocal marriages as deviants from a modal type. This case of structured perception arose from an acceptance of the current anthropological classification of societies as either patrilineal or matrilineal, and of marriage within one society as either virilocal or uxorilocal. This was by no means an isolated example. In a brilliant commentary on Deacon's discovery of a section system in Ambrym, Radcliffe-Brown shows why Rivers had failed to see this in his earlier field trip to the island. Rivers had gone there expecting to find a matrilineal dual division. 'His first enquiries showed him the existence of patrilineal local clans. He thereupon gave up looking for the matrilineal dual division, because, perhaps unconsciously, he assumed that the two forms of organisation could not exist in the same people' (Radcliffe-Brown 1929: 50). Curiously enough, Emeneau found that Rivers had also failed to record the existence of complementary descent groups among the Toda.

Fortes showed that Ashanti marriage cannot be categorized by blanket terms such as 'matrilocal' and 'patrilocal'. But he does not leave the situation merely negatively defined. 'Our investigation shows', he concludes, 'that elementary statistical procedures reduce apparently discrete "types" or "forms" of domestic organization in Ashanti to the differential effects of identical principles in varying local, social contexts' (1949(b): 84). And the particular method he uses is the same as in the Tallensi—the examination of the composition of domestic groups in relation to the stage in the growth cycle of the family. He again emphasizes the impermanence of domestic and family groups. 'Each domestic group comes into being, grows and expands, and finally dissolves' (1949(b): 60).

In one way Fortes' approach can be regarded as a synthesis of the traditions of the study of kinship deriving from Malinowski on the one hand, and Morgan and Rivers on the other. In a well-known article in *Man* (1930), Malinowski proclaims his rejection of the 'kinship algebra' school of Rivers, including the Californian trinity, Lowie, Kroeber and Gifford, and his acceptance of the 'biographical approach', which, as Fortes has pointed out in a forthcoming article (1957), derived essentially from his early work in the Westermarck tradition on the Australian family and from his interest in Freud and the importance of the 'initial situation'. Fortes' analysis of the growth cycle of domestic groups takes into account both the biographical aspects of kinship and the interrelationship of these with the permanent structure of unilineal descent groups.

For Malinowski the study of kinship began, and almost ended, with the family: 'the family is always the domestic institution *par excellence*' (1930: 23). He became the most vociferous proponent of the dogma of the universality of the family. He has been followed in recent years by Murdock in his *Social Structure* who declares the nuclear family, the equivalent of Malinowski's individual family, to be universal as a co-residential unit. Moreover it 'always has its distinctive and vital functions—sexual, economic, reproductive, and educational' (Murdock 1949: 3). The objection to Murdock's statement, apart from the fact that with respect to the family as a universal co-residential unit it is quite wrong, is that to regard every society as being composed of a number of multi-functional units called elementary, nuclear or individual is to attempt to assimilate it too closely to Euro-American patterns and to encourage gross simplifications in the analysis of domestic organization.

I have reviewed elsewhere some recent sociological literature which suffers from having followed the Malinowski–Murdock approach, in part or in whole. Here I want only to make the point that the use of the blanket term 'family' to indicate groups which are specifically defined by residence and descent as well as those defined by the existence of the marriage bond may be adequate for Euro-American systems in which there is considerable overlap, but it can be highly confusing in studies of other societies. It is significant that in speaking of the developmental cycle among the Ashanti, Fortes no longer uses the phrase 'developmental cycle of family groups' but speaks rather of domestic groups.[1] The connection between this and the Ashanti situation is plain, for co-residence is not an essential corollary of marriage, and domestic groups are in some cases constituted on non-familial lines. But it must be stressed that neither in the case of the Tallensi nor the LoDagaba does the domestic organization focus exclusively on one multi-functional unit which emerges in all domestic situations. There are a number of such units which appear in different situations. The main contexts in which they emerge are the two basic processes of production and reproduction. With the process of reproduction, in which the elementary family differentiates itself, I am not primarily concerned in this paper. It is upon the process of food production that I have concentrated and upon the groups of persons which act together in its four main phases: production, distribution, preparation and consumption. In addition I have included a section on dwelling groups, as these form the inclusive setting for these other units.

This focus of attention is connected with the general problem posed by my fieldwork. I worked among two neighbouring communities in the Northern Territories of the Gold Coast, the LoWiili and the LoDagaba, which I speak of collectively as the LoDagaa. Their cultural practices are in most respects very similar. Moreover both are characterized by dual descent, in the sense that each individual is a member of a named patriclan as well as a named matriclan. The central difference between the two communities is that whereas among the LoWiili male property is vested in the patriclan, among the LoDagaba male property is divided into two categories which I speak of as movable and immovable. The former is vested in the matriclan, and the latter in the patriclan. Thus the LoDagaba have corporate matriclans as well as corporate patriclans in the sense that each has its own 'estate', each is a property-holding corporation.

I have elsewhere related these differences to differences in ritual institutions, specifically funeral ceremonies and ancestor worship, and these again were linked to variations in nuclear kinship relations (Goody 1954). I maintained that in the community in which property was divided between the patriclan and the matriclan, or, to translate this broadly into kinship terms, between the father and the mother's brother, that in this society the relationship of a man with his father was less marked by conflict, and that with his mother's brother more so, than in the community in which all male property was vested in the patriclan. And that these differences in kinship relationships, arising from the different incidence of the holder-heir situation, were reflected in ritual ceremonies, particularly those centring around death. For death, precipitating the problem of inheritance, also precipitates the expression in customary acts of the conflicts involved in the transmission of relatively exclusive rights from one generation to the next. And the significant rights in redefining the relationships between nuclear kin, I maintained, were not rights to the membership of unilineal descent groups, as such, but rights to objects of property, in this case wealth.

In this paper I want to carry out a general examination of the process of fission of domestic groups among the LoDagaba and at the same time continue the inquiry into the variations concomitant with the differences in property relations between the LoWiili and the LoDagaba. I have concentrated upon units of production rather than reproduction, partly because it was not possible to treat both in the space, and partly because it was the former which seemed most likely to be influenced by the system of inheritance. This supposition was checked by a rough analysis of units of reproduction (i.e. elementary or compound families), the results of which are given in an appendix. There seemed to be no differences of any significance between the figures for the LoDagaba, the LoWiili and the Tallensi.

The data on these groups are partly numerical. In some cases the figures I am dealing with are small, too small perhaps to be significant in a purely statistical sense. I would stress that they are offered in confirmation of the analysis of the diachronic process whereby new groups establish themselves and old ones disappear, that is, the process of fission. There is more than one process of division which has been called fission or segmentation, for the terms have tended to be confused. What I am here concerned with is a process of replacement, cyclical fission. The following section is devoted to a general discussion of this problem.

FISSION

Since Fortes and Evans-Pritchard employed Durkheim's term 'segmentary' in connection with lineage systems there has been considerable discussion of fission and the related concept of segmentation, much of it confused or confusing. In a recent article Barnes analyses various types of segmentation occurring among the Fort Jameson Ngoni of Northern Rhodesia (1955). What he discusses is the foundation of 'primal segments', which are spatially defined groups consisting of 'diverse lineage segments' welded together into a unitary political system.

I have recently discussed the difficulties which centre around the use of the term segmentation, difficulties which inhere in the usages both of Durkheim and of Fortes and Evans-Pritchard (Goody 1957). Barnes, while making a useful distinction, has added another level of ambiguity. It is true that in a footnote he expresses his indebtedness to Mrs U. P. Mayer for the observation that his terminology differs from Fortes who 'uses "segmentation" to refer to a *state* of internal subdivision within a group and "fission" to refer to the *process* of internal subdivision'. Barnes on the other hand defines both segmentation and fission as *processes*, the former being 'the process by which any social group becomes subdivided internally and yet retains its own unity and cohesion', the latter being 'the process by which a social group divided into two or more distinct groups, so that the original group disappears as a social entity' (Barnes 1955: 20).

This distinction is a useful one and I shall return to it shortly. It is the terminology that requires a comment, for in the course of making this distinction he seems to blur an existing one whose utility has been established. In order to avoid this I shall retain Fortes' use of segmentation and take it to refer to a state of internal subdivision. But it is a particular form of internal subdivision. Segments,[2] that is, exhaustive subdivisions of a community, may be either 'simply juxtaposed so as to form a linear series' or alternatively 'involved with several others in another aggregate still more extensive, and from this series of successive involvements there results the unity of the total society' (Durkheim 1893: 178). The states of internal subdivision we may therefore distinguish as *juxtaposition* (a linear series) and *segmentation* (a merging series). But what I wish to discuss is not states but processes; that is, the fission and fusion of groups. I raise the problem of segmentation only in an attempt to clarify the discussion and to point to the background against which fission occurs.

The difficulty in studying the fission of groups is that the process only takes place over a considerable stretch of time and the anthropologist is therefore never in a position to observe even one such process in its totality. His material for reconstructing a regular developmental sequence must consist therefore of two sorts of data. First, there are the data concerning the actual state of subdivision in the community, which will include material relating to groups at all stages of development. Secondly, there are the statements of the actors themselves about the way in which subdivision takes place. The problems of analysis depend partly upon the state of internal subdivision mentioned above, but also upon the nature of the groups themselves. An elementary family exists no longer than the members themselves; clans continue from one generation to the next. Even in a linear series, therefore, the constituent segments may be thought of as perpetual, like named unilineal descent groups, or they may constantly die and be reborn, like elementary families. In the first case, it is the personnel of the group which is replaced; in the second, it is the groups themselves which are replaced. Fission has a very different meaning in each case.

In the second of these two instances, we know of course that there is a developmental cycle and the statements of the actors will provide valuable data upon it. But in the first case, we cannot tell whether or not clan A has split from clan B. Any story which the actors may tell purporting to relate to fission in the distant past may in fact be merely a charter for the existing structural situation. For example, the LoDagaba have a system of minor, major and maximal ritual areas. Many stories exist which tell how the maximal area gradually split up to form the present pattern. The anthropologist may regard these stories as accounts of fission, as indeed they purport to be, or he may look upon them as explanatory statements about the present state of segmentation. It is sociologically more sound to think of them in the second way. On the other hand unless we use such material it is difficult to make any statements about the process of fission in the case of the larger groups in the community. I believe that in the case of the LoDagaba, who appear to have moved into the area from the south, these stories are not only statements about the organization of social groups, but may well be accounts of a historical process of fission. My reason for believing the latter to be so is that the accounts given by informants appear to fit with the partial view which the anthropologist acquires of such processes at the present day.

A precisely similar situation arises in connection with stories which the LoDagaba tell of how patriclans split to form two or more linked clans. These are patently significant statements about present social relationships. But they also serve to supplement the anthropologist's observations on 'interstitial' groups by providing a skeletal framework of the process of fission.

These stories relating to fission have an additional interest. For their existence clearly shows that although major groups in the community are thought of as enduring in time, nevertheless the possibility of their growth and decay is visualized. Mechanisms such as the incorporation of close extra-clan kinsmen may in fact be consciously recognized as ways of preventing the disappearance of a particular group. I make this point because anthropologists engaged in synchronic studies have tended to overemphasize the perpetuity of a social structure through time, both from the observer's and the actor's viewpoints. Although the actors may regard the form of their society as having persisted through time, they certainly do not necessarily regard the particular constellation of social groups as being the same now as from time immemorial. Clan legends of migration and fission conceptualize this impermanency.

Just as there are two types of state of internal subdivision—juxtaposition in a linear series and segmentation in a merging series—so there are two types of fissive process which lead to these states. I call the first definitive process *fission* and the other partial process, *cleavage*. And just as there are two types of juxtaposition in a linear series—that which characterizes units like clans which are thought of as being perpetual, and that which is associated with groups such as elementary families which are recognized as being ephemeral—so there are separate types of fissive process leading to these states. This distinction is important, for in the first instance the new unit is an additional member of a linear series, while in the second the group must be considered as a replacement within the cycle of growth and decay. In order to distinguish these two processes I shall speak of the first as additive fission and the second as cyclical fission.

What I have called cleavage is what Barnes speaks of as segmentation, 'the process by which any social group becomes subdivided internally and yet retains its own unity'. This formulation is somewhat paradoxical. The process of subdivision occurs in the context of specific human actions and the group cannot in that same context be both unitary and divided. The retention of unity must be in relation to another set of activities. It is I think clear that cleavage can only be said to occur in multifunctional groups.

Single activity groups such as dwelling groups or marriage groups can only split completely (fission) never partially (cleavage). For if they are defined upon the basis of that one activity, then when the group subdivides in relation to that activity there can be no more inclusive group based upon the same criterion of eligibility. If on the other hand eligibility is based upon a general principle of association such as unilineal descent or contiguity then internal subdivision may occur at one level of the merging series and identification at the next. Indeed a genealogically defined group such as a lineage subdivides by cleavage every time a birth occurs. The result is a state of segmentation, a merging series. Maximal lineages constantly subdivide throughout their entire generation depth but this genealogical subdivision only becomes significant in the context of particular activities which must be performed by a group based upon one generation depth or, as Fortes calls it, order of segmentation, rather than another. These activity groups are of course subject to fission. For example, if a regular farming party grew too large it would split into two discrete groups, partly because there is an optimum size for these but, more important, because of the demands of reciprocity. For each of the groups is differentiated only in the context of other similar groups and between these groups a number of reciprocal services are carried on. Should, for example, the numerical composition of the groups be grossly different, one of them will suffer in the exchange system and fission may occur. But in terms of the genealogical system itself, the constituent groups will still combine at the higher orders of segmentation. Cleavage of the lineage occurs only at the minimal order, and fission only at the maximal. However we shall see that the actual point at which the fission of action groups occurs is often influenced by the lineage structure, particularly at the lower levels.

The groups dealt with in this paper are subject only to fission of a cyclical nature, not to definitive fission nor yet to cleavage. For they are essentially ephemeral, undergoing a constant process of growth and decay, dependent upon the three-generational cycle of human life and the establishment and dispersal of residential conjugal units. But the framework within which this occurs is that of unilineal descent groups, the major descent groups, or clans, and their genealogically defined subsections. Both such groups are also subject to division, even under conditions of a relatively stable population. Clans may readjust their relationships by definitive fission on the one hand, and definitive fusion on the other. This is an occasional event. But lineages are constantly subdividing, each time, in fact, that a new member is born. Here again there is a parallel process of genealogical shrinkage at some point in the structure. But these two processes of subdivision are essentially dissimilar from the fission of domestic groups.

UNITS OF PRODUCTION

This section deals with the farming group, the group of males who farm, harvest and store the main crops jointly, together with the women and children whom they support by their efforts. A comparison of the average strength of these groups in the two communities shows that among the LoWiili they are significantly larger. By an examination of the kin structure of these groups, the difference in size can be related to the differences in the relationship pattern. Fission occurs at an earlier point in the growth cycle of domestic groups among the LoDagaba than it does among the LoWiili and this fact is attributed to the different systems of property relations in the two groups, in particular to the different ways in which relatively exclusive rights over material objects are transmitted within and between generations.

An alternative to this explanation might have attributed the differences in size of these groups to different systems of production, or to the same system of production operating under different ecological conditions, or to different systems of holding rather than transmitting rights, i.e. land tenure, for example. This alternative has to be met. Yet I do not want to offer a detailed account of LoDagaba agriculture, as it is in fact basically the same as that of the other inhabitants of the Northern Territories of the Gold Coast such as the Tallensi, and even closer to that of the LoWiili which I have described in a recent book. The LoDagaba too are hoe farmers, whose principal crops are guinea-corn and millet. An early crop of maize often helps out during the hungry period before the main harvest. Groundnuts and other root crops supplement this cereal diet. However, it is not the many similarities in which I am interested, but the differences, in order to see whether any can account for the differences in the size of the productive units. I do not think they can. But first let us examine them as reported by an agricultural expert who conducted a survey in this area.

In his report J. H. Hinds (1951) presents the results of his investigations among what he calls the 'Lobi' and 'Dagarti' peoples; the former include the LoDagaba as well as the LoWiili and the DagaaWiili, while the latter are what are usually called the Dagaba. The main differences he observes are in the availability of land and the type of farm preferred. With regard to the first factor, this is related to the density of the population. The 1948 census gives the density for the whole of the Lawra Administrative District as eighty-one persons per square mile. This District includes all the groups mentioned above. Within the District, however, there is considerable internal variation in density. The western areas inhabited by the 'Lobi' of Hinds (whom I call collectively the LoDagaa) are much more thickly populated than the eastern part in which the Dagaba live. The point is made more emphatically when it is recalled that the density of the neighbouring districts of Wa to the south (mainly Dagaba) and Tumu to the east are twenty-five and eleven to the square mile respectively.

The differences Hinds noted between the LoDagaa ('Lobi') and the Dagaba occur also, though to a lesser extent, within the former, that is, between the LoWiili and the LoDagaba. My point is that these central differences depend not primarily upon different cultural traditions, as Hinds appears to assume, but upon the relative densities of population. The inhabitants of the LoWiili settlement of Birifu are thickly scattered on the ground and what land there is suffers from laterite formation and soil erosion. Their fields are largely situated in and around the inhabited area. Nearly all are continuously cropped and therefore have to be manured in order to maintain a reasonable yield. In its turn this continuous cropping leads to increased erosion and this further decreases the land available for cultivation.

In the LoDagaba settlement of Tom the situation is quite different. The dwellings themselves are distributed about as evenly over the inhabited areas as are those in Birifu. The ground within a few yards of the compound (*seman*) is equally important to the inhabitants of both these settlements. It has a high fertility due to the quantity of human detritus which finds its way there and the crops sown there are interspersed with the vegetables planted by the women for the preparation of sauces. But whereas most farming in Birifu is carried on in the home farms within and immediately around the inhabited area, the LoDagaba of Tom prefer to make their main farms in the bush, where they can allow the land to lie idle when the yields begin to drop more than a certain amount. [3]

The settlement of Tom is particularly well favoured as far as land is concerned. About two miles to the south the river Kambaa runs westwards towards the Black Volta. The spread of sleeping sickness since the end of the last century, assisted by the presence of blindness caused by water-borne carriers, led to an exodus from the Kambaa Valley. Land is plentiful and is now available to those living in the remaining settlements which, like Tom, are mainly situated on the high ground some distance from the river banks themselves. The land immediately round the compounds is certainly highly valued but the better yields from fallow land are clearly recognized.

I want to emphasize that the preference of the LoDagaa for compound farms and the Dagaba for bush farms is not primarily a question of cultural differences. When LoWiili migrate to more open parts they too prefer to make a farm in the bush and abandon it when the yield drops. European writers tend to regard continuous cultivation as the most advanced form of agriculture. In these circumstances it is not necessarily the most rewarding, over either a short or a long term. Table I, which is based on Hinds' figures shows that larger yields are obtained in the community in which shifting cultivation is more common.

Table 1. *Guinea-corn yields per acre*

Weighted means for the period 1941–5.

	Pounds per acre	
	Unmanured	Manured
LoDagaa	320	524
Dagaba	425	612

These figures also show the advantages of manuring, which is much more prevalent among the LoDagaa as against the Dagaba, and the LoWiili as against the LoDagaba. Thus it in part compensates for the greater dependence upon permanent compound farms. Indeed manure is rarely carried to distant bush farms. But although the compound farmers manure to a greater extent, their supplies of cowdung and human detritus are limited and they are unable to treat much of their farmland as heavily as is required to gain any substantial increase in yield. Consequently they recognize that its use can be no complete substitute for shifting cultivation.

A further advantage in not using manure is that a man can then hand over his cattle to one of the Fulani who have penetrated the area from the north-west. This no LoWiili does, as he requires the manure. But among the LoDagaba in Tom, there are three elementary families of Fulani who look after the great bulk of the cattle. They are much better at this than the local populace who tend to regard it as an occupation for small boys. These Fulani require no payment; they merely retain the milk, which the LoDagaa anyhow leave to small boys and puppies, and the dung, which they only use when conditions demand.

The differences in the agricultural practices of the LoWiili and the LoDagaba are principally a function of the availability of resources. A man from either group migrating to a populated area will become primarily a home farmer, a man moving to the thinly scattered regions will adopt the Dagaba type of bush farming.

These differences in productive methods do not demand any major differences in productive relations. The method of defining rights in land, the basic productive resource, is similar in both cases, although the degree of precision with which these are defined varies with the density of habitation. There is little difference in the crops sown and the tools used. The methods of organizing labour are similar in both cases. Most of the work in respect of the crops of major importance is done by groups of men either fulfilling the affinal obligations of one of their number or else working in turn upon each other's farms. These groups consist of neighbours who are also usually agnatic kinsfolk. Communal farming parties are more in evidence among the LoDagaba than among the LoWiili and more of the farm work is carried out by this means. This may be related to the fact that the former cultivate a larger area of land per person. According to Hinds, the acreage farmed per person sustained was as follows:

	Acreage per person
LoWiili	0·9 (76 persons)
LoDagaba	1·5 (76 persons)
Dagaba	1·8 (125 persons)

Thus the LoDagaba more nearly approach the figures of the patrilineal Dagaba, their neighbours to the east. Not only is there more work, but it is also more arduous, the farms being situated at some distance in the middle of thick scrubland infested with wild animals. Communal farming not only ensures that arduous work is carried out in relatively congenial conditions, it promotes continuous application by establishing a system of reciprocities. And it produces not only longer but greater effort by its competitive nature.

An area to be farmed is divided into the same number of strips (*ne*, lit. mouths) as there are farmers present. Each man is allotted a strip and the one who succeeds in finishing his first bursts into victory halloos. Considerable prestige is attached to one's ability as a farmer. Indeed the victory cry is similar to that given in the hunt when a wild animal has been killed.

It is reasonable to suppose that the greater stress on communal farming is functionally related to the greater acreage of land farmed by each member of the community. It might be supposed that this difference would also militate in favour of a larger unit of production. For although the actual agricultural activities are carried out mainly by farming parties, the effective unit of production is a much smaller unit, consisting of a small group of agnates and their wives, a father and his sons, a group of siblings, who share joint farming rights over a particular area of ground in which their main crops are grown, who farm this area together with the exception of a few individual plots for subsidiary crops such as groundnuts and possibly other root crops which are often sold for cash, and who store the produce in one granary. It is the senior male member of this group who is responsible for allocating the grain among the women attached to it.

A comparison of the composition of these groups shows a considerable and highly significant difference between the LoWiili and the LoDagaba. The average strength of the unit of production among these groups is shown in Table 2.

Table 2. *Average strength of the unit of production*

(The figures in brackets show the numbers in the sample.)

	Men	Women	Children	Total
LoWiili	2·50*	3·3	5·3	11·1
(46 units)	(114)	(153)	(243)	(510)
LoDagaba	1·5†	2·8	3·3	7·0
(48 units)	(75)	(104)	(159)	(338)

* This figure includes youths 0·22 and incapacitated 0·11.
† This figure includes incapacitated 0·04.

The number of individuals in a LoWiili farming group is considerably larger, but it is the difference in the number of men in these groups which is of particular interest. Table 3 shows the frequency of adult males per farming group in the two communities.

Thus among the LoWiili, 60% of all units of production were joint farming groups, that is, contained more than one adult male, whereas among the LoDagaba only 27% of the groups had this form. This indeed is a striking difference between the two communities. It means, in developmental terms, that fission of the farming group occurs at an earlier stage among the LoDagaba than among the LoWiili. In both societies of course each individual

65

begins farming with his father and his elder brothers. A smaller farming group means therefore in developmental terms that the fission of this group takes place at an earlier stage in the growth cycle of domestic groups.

Table 3. *Adult males in farming groups*

	0	1	2	3	4	5	8	Total males
LoWiili (50 units)	2	18	16	10	2	1	1	101
LoDagaba (59 units)	5	32	7	9	0	0	0	79

A larger number of units appears in Table 3 than in Table 2. This is because in arriving at the average composition of the farming group I excluded certain types of group. These are listed below:

	Groups with no adult males			Groups with incapacitated males			
	No.	Women	Children	No.	Men	Women	Children
LoWiili	2	2	2	2	2	0	0
LoDagaba	5	6	25	6	6	3	6

These figures have been excluded from Table 2 and included in Table 3. Excluded from the category adult males in Table 3, however, are the youths and incapacitated which I have included in Table 2, that is to say, ten youths and five incapacitated in the LoWiili sample and two incapacitated in the LoDagaba sample. Had I included these in Table 3 this would have increased the number of joint units among the former. I decided not to include them owing to the fact that I dispensed with the category 'youths' in the LoDagaba survey and in reallocating these between adults and children I might have been influenced by the case I was making.

It must of course be borne in mind that as the process of fission is a three-generational one, the age-structure of the adult males in the LoDagaba sample may be significantly different from that of the LoWiili. Furthermore, as my criterion of adulthood in default of others is based upon marriageable age this also may differ in the two communities. In the absence of precise data upon ages, I have to rely on my own estimates of a normal distribution. Given similar normal distributions in the two societies, the size of the sample would appear to set aside the first objection. With regard to the second, I again have only estimates of the modal age of marriage; this I would reckon as eighteen for both communities. There may be a slight tendency to earlier marriage among the LoDagaba but I do not believe that this would influence the figures to any appreciable extent. In any case by omitting the category 'youths' from Table 3 I have more than compensated for this possibility.

Among the LoWiili there were thirty joint farming groups in a total of fifty, among the LoDagaba seventeen in a total of fifty-eight. In the first community 83 % of the men farmed together with another adult male; in the second only 52 % did so.

It would be possible to frame an explanation of these facts in terms of the differences in personal inclination or differences in ethos. The first would be in terms of individual psychology, the second in terms of patterns of culture, or pattern variables. In this instance, both these types of explanation are circular. Indeed they are not explanations at all but only ways of stating the same fact at another level of abstraction. The statement that the LoWiili and LoDagaba each have their own ethos, their own cultural tradition, is of little value for analytic purposes and it is clearly inappropriate in this context. What we require is an analysis of the actual concomitants of this difference.

In order to do this, I shall first examine the relational as distinct from the numerical structure of the joint farming groups. Table 4 expresses the kinship position of the adult males in these groups in relation to their senior member.

Table 4. *The kin structure of joint farming groups* [4]

	LoWiili		LoDagaba	
Ego farming with	Units (30)	%	Units (17)	%
Sons	4		7	
Younger sons	1		2 } 9	53
Sister's illegitimate son	1 } 10	33		
Brother's sons	3			
Son and brother's son	1			
Full-brother	11		8	47
Full-brother plus	6 } 20	67		
Half-brother	2			
Other agnates	1			

It is clear from this table that in terms of the relationships of adult males, there are two modal types of productive unit, the group of full siblings and the group consisting of the father and his sons. These types, which we may speak of as the fraternal and the paternal, are to be found in all patrilineal agricultural societies, and it would be possible to classify these societies on the basis of the proportions of each of these types existing in each society.

But these groups are not stable over a long period. They are constantly hiving off one from another to form groups of another type, while at the same time other groups, often the rump segments left by the process of fission, disappear altogether. The sequence is part of the domestic cycle, the process of household development. The groups which the anthropologist examines synchronically in the field have to be analysed in terms of a developmental process, the limiting feature of which is the three-generational span of human life.

The differences in incidence and composition of joint units of production must be viewed in terms of this developmental process. For even those farming groups which consist of one adult male are in a wider sense composite units of production. In his hoeing tasks a man is assisted by his sons as soon as they can wield a hoe, often as early as 8 years of age. In addition the women have their own productive tasks. They are the proper persons to sow the seed, a task which is associated with their role as childbearers. They always grow

67 5-2

their own vegetables for sauces in the fertile patch immediately around the homestead, and they also assist in the harvest. Among the LoDagaba the younger of them sometimes organize a party to farm for a mother's brother or for a lover.

It is the group of adult males, however, which is the main focus of interest in discussing production. Table 4 indicates a wider genealogical span of agnates in the LoWiili sample. In this community one finds a certain number of men farming with half-brothers and with their dead brother's sons whereas the LoDagaba groups are entirely confined to the two main types. What is the reason for this? Why should a LoDagaba be less likely to farm with his agnatic kinsfolk than a LoWiili? Or to put the question in developmental terms, why does fission occur at an earlier stage in LoDagaba farming groups? For a clearer idea of the process of fission, we must turn to an examination of the occasions in which we find full siblings and fathers and sons farming separately. This is shown in Table 5.

Table 5. *The fission of paternal and fraternal farming groups*

| | Split father-son farming groups | | | |
	Eldest son only farms apart	All or only sons farm apart	Joint father-son farming groups	Total father-son units in sample
LoDagaba	2	2	7	11
LoWiili	1	0	5	6

| | Split full brother farming groups | | | |
	All full brothers farm individually	Pairs of full brothers farm apart	Joint full brother farming groups	Total full brother units in sample
LoDagaba	5*	1	6	12
LoWiili	2	0	17	19

* This includes one sibling group of five members, each of whom farms on his own: I have counted this as one instance.

The number of such groups is too small to permit definite statements on this basis alone. But when these data are considered side by side with the actor's own idea of the process of fission it can be seen to indicate the general trend. In the first place sons are more often found farming on their own among the LoDagaba than among the LoWiili. Indeed the LoWiili example was an exceptional case and recognized by the people as such. I myself knew of no similar instance. The LoDagaba examples were not exceptional nor were they thought of as such by the people themselves.

For groups of full siblings the position is clearer. There is a definite trend towards earlier fission among the LoDagaba.

The analysis of the numerical data has set the problem, to explain the numerical differences in productive units among the LoWiili and the Lo-Dagaba. It has carried the analysis a stage further by indicating that in the second case the fission of such groups occurs at an earlier stage in the domestic cycle both in paternal and in fraternal groups. It is not only a question of eldest sons breaking away from fathers to set up their own independent productive units, but also of full brothers separating at an earlier stage in the developmental cycle of domestic groups.

The earlier fission of farming groups among the LoDagaba might appear to result from greater tension between agnates. Were this so, it should also be reflected in the dwelling groups, but as we shall see this is not in fact the case. It would, moreover, contradict the evidence on the relationships between nuclear kin which were outlined in the introductory section. Indeed it indicates just the opposite.

When the LoDagaba are asked about the split between sons and fathers, they will reply, 'it's the matriclan (*belo*)'. In fact it is not the existence of matriclanship itself which could be responsible for the difference, for both communities have this institution. Rather it is the matrilineal inheritance of wealth (*gbandiru*). The LoDagaba are quite explicit about this process. They say that a father will deliberately oust ('*o*) his senior son for his own good, keeping the junior son to farm with him. As I have mentioned, this statement usually refers to groups of full siblings rather than to individuals. The reason is this. When a man dies, his wealth is inherited by a member of his matriclan, and because of the rule of exogamy this can never be one of his sons. If therefore the sons continue to farm with their father, they will certainly fill his granaries and give him a good surplus which he can sell and use to buy livestock. But when he dies, this surplus is claimed by the uterine heir and the sons have no claim on the goods which have been bought with the sweat of their brows. Consequently it is of advantage to the sons to have their own granaries and to build up their own flocks. Their father will encourage them to do this when he considers the time has come. But the youngest son will be expected to stay with his father as the prop to his old age. In return, he will receive extra gifts while his father lives, and the central granary when he is dead. Preferential ultimogeniture is here, as often, a form of old age insurance.

One old man I knew well, Kūbiu, had ten adult sons, five pairs of full siblings.[5] Each pair of full siblings formed a separate farming group, the junior pair farming with their father. As a result of this early fission, at Kūbiu's death the uterine heir would be entitled only to the wealth accumulated by the one farming group, and to the contents of one granary. It is not surprising therefore to find among the LoDagaba sample no case where paternal half-brothers or more distant agnates farmed together. For if a member of such a group died, one of his uterine kinsmen would become entitled to his share of the joint property, which would then pass out of the group's control.

There was none of the open hostility between Kŭbiu and the sons farming separately from him that was plain to everyone in the one LoWiili case of a father-son split that I knew. This was in Bŏyiri's compound, which was very similar in composition to that of Kŭbiu. Bŏyiri farmed with his five adult sons—by three different mothers—and two adult sister's sons. But his eldest son, San, had been ousted and farmed alone. There was great bitterness between them, of which the whole settlement was well aware.

The implications of ousting are quite different in the two communities. I do not mean to imply by this that relationships between LoDagaba fathers and sons are free of conflict. They are not. I have heard a father threaten to cut a boy off because he was not giving him enough help on the farm. But this threat only had force because the boy was in his teens and could not have managed on his own. To an adult it would have been no threat at all, because it is no disgrace among the LoDagaba to farm apart from one's father. Indeed he encourages it.

In this case, the LoDagaba father claimed the son had been spending too much time on farming parties which never came to help on his own farm. Among the LoWiili only farming for one's father-in-law is not reciprocal. Among the LoDagaba, on the other hand, a person is expected by his mother's brother to bring a hoeing party to his farm every now and again. It is supposedly in return for this assistance that the mother's brother supplies the brideprice for a man's second wife, though in fact he also receives half the brideprice given at the marriage of his sister's daughter. If therefore the sister's son does no work for his mother's brother, he may not get the bride-price; this is the recognized sanction. There is thus a whole further category of non-reciprocal hoeing parties in which a man engages on his own behalf. If a son spends too much time on these parties (and because of their communal character and the food and drink provided they are often more of an attraction than working at home), his father will feel that the boy might just as well be farming by himself and providing his own food and clothing. Equally the son, belonging as he does to a different wealth-holding corporation from the father, will prefer to spend his time building up his own independent resources, knowing that he has no claim on those of his father after the father's death. Farming for one's mother's brother is one aspect of this. Another is migratory labour. Much of the manual labour in the south of the Gold Coast is provided by the young men from the north who go down after the harvest and return in time for the next farming season. Among the LoWiili such labour is very largely of a seasonal nature. A young man goes south, earns some money and returns with his purchases, which he then offers to his father. And whatever his father chooses to take, he knows it will be his in due course. The LoDagaba have the same system of offering one's gains to the father, but the difference here is that a man is aware that whatever his father takes will be inherited not by himself but by another.

My figures on the extent of labour migration among the LoDagaba are not sufficiently reliable for a profitable comparison with the LoWiili data. But it is my strong impression that among the former trips are made more frequently, for a longer duration and by a larger proportion of the inhabitants. This I suggest is related to the desire of sons to build up their own resources independent of their fathers. Certainly from the actor's point of view, migrant labour is much more strongly entrenched as a means of making money. The LoDagaba themselves account for the cases of full brothers farming independently of one another by the institution of migrant labour. One of the five cases given in Table 5 consisted of five full brothers each farming on their own. These men were in their thirties and had this been a LoWiili compound I would certainly have expected to find them farming together. The trouble was, they told me, that one member of a farming group would go off to work in the south and then might decide to stay during the following wet season. Thus the other members of the farming group would be left to provide for his wife and children, a situation which could only lead to conflict.

The earlier split between agnates who are not uterine kin is clearly related to the system of inheritance. While there is no direct reason why this should cause earlier fission in groups of full siblings, the system of inheritance does in fact place a premium upon a young man's setting up an independent fund, and in order to achieve this end he spends more time as a migrant labourer. The difficulties created by this appear to lead to the earlier fission between full brothers.

In general, then, the difference in the size of farming groups in the two communities is to be related to difference in systems of property relations rather than in the productive systems themselves. Indeed methods of gaining a livelihood are very similar. What differences there are, namely the larger bush farms among the LoDagaba, would appear to favour a larger farming group whereas in fact we find smaller ones. This elimination of the productive system as a factor in these differences is confirmed by figures given by Hinds for the strengths of farming groups in this area. For he includes a sample from the neighbouring Dagaba which serves as a check on the data we have presented. These figures are shown in Table 6.

Table 6. *Strength of farming groups and acreage farmed*

	Adult men per group	Total persons per group	Acreage farmed per person	Total number of persons
LoWiili	2·9	10·9	0·9	71
LoDagaba	2·6	8·4	1·5	76
Dagaba	3·3	10·4	1·8	125

The total numbers of persons involved are smaller than in the case of my LoWiili and LoDagaba samples. For this and other reasons I think that my own figures are more accurate. The same difference in the size of the farming groups in these two communities appears in Hinds' figures. But what most strikingly confirms the analysis I have presented is the Dagaba data. For the Dagaba live in a comparatively sparsely populated area and therefore have the same opportunity as the LoDagaba to cultivate bush farms. This they do and the acreage farmed per person sustained is similar among these two groups. But despite this similarity in the productive systems the total numbers of persons per farming group differs considerably. The patrilineally inheriting Dagaba and the patrilineally inheriting LoWiili are the ones which are similar in this respect, although their productive systems, at least in terms of acreage farmed, are the most dissimilar. It is the LoDagaba, the only group to inherit wealth matrilineally, who differ significantly in this respect. The average strength of the farming group is considerably smaller, and it is the reasons behind this earlier fission that I have been investigating in this section.

UNITS OF CONSUMPTION

In this section I shall examine the process whereby the grain in the granary reaches the bellies of the members of the society. This may be broken down into three phases: distribution, preparation and consumption.

The system of food distribution among the LoDagaba differs somewhat from that of the LoWiili. Among the former a woman is less dependent upon her husband because although she acquires the greater part of her supplies from him in the same way, she does so in larger quantities. A regular feature of the LoDagaba houses is the woman's granary wherein a wife places the grain she has been given. Her main supplies come from her husband at harvest time but she also receives food independently from other sources as well.

When a girl is about to be married, she goes round her 'mothers' (*mamine*) and her 'mother's brothers' (*madebmine*), that is, senior members of her own matriclan and her mother's patriclan 'siblings', and asks them for various household necessities. From the males, she gets 'men's things', rice, grain, yams, groundnuts, perhaps some money. From the women, she will get 'women's things', earthenware pots and bowls, gourds for drinking vessels, and shea-nut butter, dawa-dawa flour and nuts, and red peppers.[6] The objects which a woman acquires from men, she possesses in her own right, but cannot transmit to other women at her death; they are tied to the male sex. The objects she receives from women are the utensils in which she stores and cooks the food and the ingredients she uses to prepare the sauces which invariably accompany the basic cereal dish. Both these categories of objects she acquires not from her agnates with whom she lives but from her matri-lateral and matrilineal kinsfolk. In just the same way a boy is set up by his 'mother's brother' both as a warrior and as a property holder. It is the 'mother's brothers' who fill his first quiver with arrows and his mother's nearest brother who provides him with a fowl (*no hgwəl*) from which by careful husbandry he may breed chickens to sell in the market.

The foundation of a woman's own property is laid by her matrilineal and matrilateral kin. When she is married she receives nothing from her father. But at each subsequent guinea-corn harvest she will return to her father's house, help them cut the corn and take away with her as much corn as she can carry, as much that is as the largest basket will hold. And if she is ever in need she can go back to her father's house and ask for food to feed her children. This she has to ask for. No child can go to his father's granary, unless specifically told to go. But it is recognized that while this would be unforgivable for a son, daughters are liable to sneak inside and steal (*zu*) some grain.

These are additional supplies of grain which help to give a wife a certain amount of economic independence. She may use the grain to make food or to brew beer for sale. By this means she can eventually become quite wealthy. This would not happen until she becomes an old woman, having shed her responsibilities to her children, and possibly to her husband as well. For such a woman has her son's wife to perform all the domestic tasks which formerly occupied her day. She can now 'sit and rest' with ample time for brewing beer and trading in the various weekly markets in the surrounding settlements.

Although a woman will try and keep her wealth apart, in the last resort she will always use it to feed her husband, and more particularly her children, if the husband has been unable to provide sufficient for them. Nevertheless what she acquired by these means is conceptually quite separate from the 'woman's grain' (*pobo tʃi*) which a husband gives to his wife after the harvest. This consists of the heads of guinea corn which have not fully ripened (*kazaari*) as well as the whole of the millet crop. [7]

This system differs from that of the LoWiili. There it is most unusual to find a woman's granary, although she does of course have various pots of her own in which she keeps subsidiary crops such as beans and groundnuts. The grain itself, however, is retained in the hands of the men who make regular distributions to their wives throughout the year. Among the LoDagaba on the other hand a man gives a woman quite a sizeable proportion and this has to last her through the dry season. Indeed, a good, careful woman can make it last much longer. The length of time the group lives upon the contents of the woman's granary depends of course not only on her housekeeping abilities but on how much her husband has been able to provide in the first place. If he has had a really poor harvest he will retain all the grain in the central store and distribute it at regular intervals as long as it lasts. In Daya's house there was no woman's granary. He had no one helping him except one small boy and he himself had been able to farm very little owing to an injury received when trying to drive an elephant from his farm. Consequently his resources were very limited and he had to husband them as best he could.

In normal times and in normal households, the LoDagaba do not make regular distributions from the central granary until the beginnings of the rains, that is, when the next planting season is under way. This distribution may take place either once or twice a week. Additional supplies have to be provided for visiting farming parties. These distributions vary in frequency and in size according to the state of the granary in question. They depend not only on directly balancing consumption against production, but also upon what saleable surplus a man aims to have by the time the next harvest comes round. Now that a number of European consumer goods are available in local markets and town stores there appears to be an increasing trend towards acquiring such a surplus.

The grain a woman is given in the first and subsequent distributions she cannot sell, as she can the grain acquired from other sources. Nor may she use it to brew beer for sale. Such an act would endanger the husband and it is said that if he were to eat anything bought with this money he would die. The sale of household resources falls in the same category as the sale of sexual services. Should the husband profit however indirectly from such transactions he is said 'to eat cheaply' (*dire mwɔre*) and will die as a result, whether the act is committed with or without his knowledge. Both the productive and reproductive processes are protected by essentially similar supernatural sanctions. These sanctions fall upon the man rather than the woman who has actually committed the sin. For as a female she is a jural minor, under the guardianship of her husband. And as a wife she is by definition a member of a patrilineage other than that in which the productive and reproductive resources are vested. Hence it is her husband who is primarily endangered by the alienation of the produce and resources.

The grain cannot be sold. It must be used to feed the members of the cooking group. On the other hand, the woman does have the right to take the grain with her should she return to her father's house. To this extent the husband, and in the case of death his kinsfolk, have alienated their rights over this produce to the wife. This means that she can provide for her children, the most junior members of the patrilineal descent group, even if she returns to her natal home or marries another man; for if they are young they will always follow their mother, whether the husband rejects his wife or she leaves him. There are two aspects of this situation I wish to emphasize. First, the transfer of control to the wife, and secondly, the fact that the core of the unit of consumption consists of a matrisegment, a mother and her children, while the core of the unit of production consists of a patrisegment, a man and his children.

Before I elaborate this point and attempt to show why this alienation should occur, I want to offer some more details on the distribution, preparation and consumption of food.

The food is distributed to all wives equally, regardless of the number of children each may have. Among the LoWiili, on the other hand, the senior woman in each cooking group is given an amount of grain which varies directly with the composition of the unit. This appears a somewhat curious difference between the two communities. But as the LoDagaba explained to me, there were ways of compensating for the apparent inequalities. When each wife prepares a meal she sends food to her husband and also to his mother if she is alive. The husband eats his daily meal on his own roof together with his adolescent sons. The girls and younger children eat with their mothers although the boys will probably all eat together from the same bowl as soon as they start farming or herding cattle. The male in a polygamous household will receive a bowl of food from his wives each time they cook. [8] The adolescent boys automatically share his food and some he may give to any children he thinks are not getting as much as the others. In this manner he evens out the inequalities in the distribution of grain. [9]

I have spoken as if each woman married into the homestead received her own allocation of grain and formed the nucleus of a distinct unit of food preparation. This is not in fact the case. Women group themselves together and take turns at cooking. When a young man first marries, his bride comes to live with him in the same room as his mother. She is under her mother-in-law's care and supervision and makes food at her direction. A room will probably not be built for her before she has borne her first child. Even then she continues to cook with her mother-in-law until a younger daughter-in-law is available. She will also cook on her own if her husband begins to farm independently of his father, for then the women will be attached to different farming groups, and therefore to different sources of grain.

Cooking groups therefore only occur within farming groups, but they do not correspond to them in terms of membership. A young wife has an obligation to perform cooking duties for her mother-in-law but none for a co-wife, nor for the wife of any of her husband's siblings with whom he may be farming (*yentaa*, co-wife, wife of husband's 'brothers'). I know of no case where the wives of two brothers cook together, even though they are members of the same unit of production. Even the co-wives of one man no longer prepare food jointly when they both have children eating solid food. It is true that if a man marries again, the second wife, if she is a young bride, will begin by helping the senior wife, just as the latter had begun by helping her mother-in-law. But this arrangement does not continue for long. 'Men can always

eat together', the LoDagaba say, 'it's women that can't.' This is understand-
able as the men who live in the same house are usually closely related to one
another whereas the women are unlikely to have any pre-existing tie of such
a nature between them. But in fact fission rarely occurs merely because two
women cannot prepare food together. Indeed if one of the women is barren
the co-wives may continue indefinitely to cook together. Women do not
divide over the distribution of food between themselves, nor yet to their
husband. On the contrary they are solidary in the face of male complaints
about food, and at sowing time when they do not get back from the bush farms
until late in the evening they may well join together in refusing to make a
cooked meal. [10] What divides the wives is the distribution of food among
their children. A cooking group is likely to split when the second wife begins
to wean her first child, or rather to offer the alternative of solid food.

The LoDagaba like the LoWiili are quite explicit about this. When the
grain is distributed it is ground up by the younger girls on a granite slab (*nier*).
In every house there is at least one such slab owned by one of the senior
women. In the planting season, the women prepare only a little porridge (*saab
kpõ*) at a time, sufficient just for the one meal. At this season I have heard
some of the older men complain of not having had a square meal for weeks
and of having to get by on beer, groundnuts and oddments bought in the
market. However, the younger men get better fed as they are the ones to turn
out on farming parties.

At less busy times of the year, the women use the grain to prepare a 'large
meal' (*saab kpẽẽ*). Some of this is eaten at the time but the porridge which
remains is put in a pot containing 'sour water' (*kwõ miiru*) which preserves
it fresh for several days. On the following days this is served cold together
with a different relish. As in the diets of most primitive communities the
major carbohydrate constituent remains basically the same and variety is
achieved through the addition of garnishes.

In each cooking group there is one storage pot for cooked food. This
represents the female equivalent of the male granary. It is a bad husband who
puts his hand in his wife's pot, just as it is a bad wife who takes grain from
the granary without specific orders. [11] This was illustrated by one house in
Tom I knew well. There were no adult males living there, just two widows
with their children, forming two very weak farming groups. They did not
produce much grain and towards the end of July the woman of one of these
farming groups went off to her father's house some fifty miles away to see if
she could beg some grain. She left her children under the care of the eldest,
a girl of sixteen. This girl had great difficulty in controlling her younger
brothers. When she was grinding corn, they would snatch the flour. Sometimes at night they would sneak into the granary and take some grain. But
worst of all they would dip their hands into the storage pot to get some

porridge. Even if a man is starving, he should never do this. For the woman who owns the pot always puts a curse on it (*o ŋmen nuɔr yoŋ*). It was for this reason people said that these youngsters would never grow into proper men (*nie*). As their elder sister used to remark, 'You can't do anything with them.' (*be be tera gwəlue*).

The cooked food kept in this storage pot is used to supply the wants of the children when they are hungry. From its earliest years, a child is given the breast whenever it cries. After the child has been weaned, the mother still tries to satisfy its wants by offering it titbits of food whenever it cries. As the only regular meal is in the evening, this may involve going to the storage pot and taking some of the cold porridge. It is in this way, the LoDagaa say, that quarrels arise between co-wives. If the other woman in the group is out at the time she may return to find nothing to give her own children. The male interpretation of the fission of cooking groups is therefore misleading. These split not because women can never under any circumstances co-operate together but because they each have a responsibility towards their own children. For despite the tensions between them inherent in a polygynous situation, childless women do cook together. A cooking partnership tends to break up when women have children of their own who have begun to eat solid foods.

This process of fission of units of consumption can be seen at work in a large homestead such as that of Nibe, the head man of the southern sector of Tom (*Zendaagō*). With him live his three full brothers and his paternal half-brother. They had built this house when their father died and had at first farmed together but now each brother farms on his own. Nibe has five wives all of whom cook separately. Two of them have newly married sons whose wives assist them. The remaining three each have several children of their own. Another of Nibe's brothers has two wives, one with six children, the other with an infant and her own younger sister who looks after the child. These wives also cook separately. Nibe's other three brothers each have two wives, and only one child among them all. In these last three cases, the co-wives share cooking duties.

Before concluding this section I want to return to the question of explaining the differences in the methods of distributing grain in the two communities. This it will be recalled was held to account for the existence of women's granaries among the LoDagaba and their absence among the LoWiili. The greater quantity of grain initially placed under the control of the cooking group requires adequate facilities for storage. Hence in addition to the central granary in which the supplies of the farming group, or unit of production, are kept, there are other smaller granaries for the grain which has been distributed to the cooking groups. The central granary is literally central, while the women's granaries are built on the outside wall, near to the open courtyard of the house.

Earlier in this section this difference was noted but not explained. The question of why larger quantities of grain should be placed in the control of LoDagaba women is not merely a random variation for the ethnographic record. It has a functional relationship to the other features of the social system. The smaller farming groups among the LoDagaba have already been attributed to the fact that while productive resources are vested in the patriclan, wealth—that is, the surplus of production over consumption—is vested in the matriclan. When a man dies, the land he farms, the implements with which he farms, the house built on the land, the shrines, ancestral and medicinal, associated with the house and its occupants, all these pass to agnatic kinsmen. In contrast to these immovables, the movable objects are inherited by the next uterine kinsmen. These consist of his money and his livestock (Goody 1954). Both these items are regarded by the LoDagaa as being acquired ultimately by the sale of the grain from the previous year which remains in the central granary of the farming group when the next harvest is gathered in. It represents the surplus of production over consumption. The heir to the movable property indeed claims the whole of the contents of the granary when a man dies. He has a right to it all and if he is a 'bad' person (*ni faa*) he may in fact sell the lot and keep the proceeds. This would not occur if the heir was a full sibling, but it could happen if the dead man was the last male in the sibling group, for the wealth would then pass to his sister's son, a member of another patrilineal descent group. A 'good' man (*ni vla*) would not behave in this way. He would leave sufficient to support the widows and orphans until the next harvest. But not all men display this generosity and handing over control of a larger amount of grain to the wife serves to protect her and the children from such an eventuality. For once it has been handed to the woman and become part of the supplies of the unit of consumption it no longer forms part of the property of the matrilineal descent group in which the wealth is vested and to which the dead man and his uterine heir, but not his widow nor his children, belong.

In concluding this section let me return to the composition of the units of consumption. It is the cooking groups, the units of food preparation, which form the basis of the internal differentiation of the units of food production (farming groups) as far as the process of distribution, preparation and consumption of food is concerned. At times, however, the group which emerges may be a larger one than this. During the farming season, particularly when a party of 'in-laws' are coming to hoe, the whole farming group may act as a unit of food preparation. On other ceremonial occasions, it may be the whole compound (*yir*) or even the members of several adjacent houses of the same patrilineage (*yir*) who both prepare and consume the food together. Indeed a saying sometimes used as a way of expressing the relationships of the members of the local section of a dispersed patriclan is 'we all have one hoe'.

This statement refers to the rights over land which a man has as member of such a group and the common interests of all members in the productive process. But how far this expression of common interests in land reflects the actual interdependence of households in times of food shortage it is difficult to say. It seems less shameful to beg (*zele*) from matrilateral connections than to seek help from one's own agnates.

The differentiation of cooking groups follows the lines of genealogical differentiation because it tends to establish mother-child units as the basic unit of consumption, even after the stage of oral dependency. Cooking units are essentially matrifocal groups to which the husband is attached in a similar sense to the way in which women are attached to the units of production. Clearly the husband's participation cannot be so strong as he may be attached to more than one of these groups concurrently.

This peripheral position of the male *vis-à-vis* the unit of consumption is quite clear when one sees how meals are eaten. When a man eats he always does so separately from his wife. She sits with the small children down in the long room while he remains on the roof-top above the room of his senior wife. Those boys who have reached the age when they can take part in farming activities also eat apart from their mothers, but not, in most households, with the adult males.

Attention has been drawn by writers such as Firth (1936) and Fortes (1945) to the crystallization of matrisegments (the children of one woman) within the patrilineage. This has usually been considered as a matter of kinship, in terms of motherhood. I have been concerned to emphasize the function of the first-order matrisegment [12] as a unit of consumption. Initially the group emerges in relation to the mother as supplier. But this physiologically determined group continues to be relevant as the core of the unit of consumption when the children are no longer orally dependent upon their mother. Social factors give it a temporal extension in terms of the life cycle. The father becomes the supplier from the point of view of production, but the mother retains her central position in the unit of consumption.

DWELLING UNITS

The last type of domestic group with which I wish to deal is the dwelling group, the occupants of one homestead. [13] Among the LoDagaa this group serves some of the same general functions as among the Tallensi. It acts as one of the principal ceremonial and jural units. Its ritual functions are partly connected with the fact that ancestor shrines are aggregated in the byre on a homestead basis and it is only through the senior member of a dwelling group that a man can offer a sacrifice to his paternal ancestors. Like other homestead shrines, these serve to protect all the people whom the dwelling shelters as a whole, not merely individually. One of the most important of these other shrines is that which is buried in the entrance to the byre. When the house is built three stones are taken from the local earth shrine and are buried there together with the faeces of children and of the beasts which will dwell there. The interests of all the occupants, human and non-human, are identified. Thus the byre houses the two main homestead shrines, the Earth and the ancestors, which form the focal points of the religious systems of the region. And just as the dwelling group frequently forms a ritual unit in worship of the ancestors, so it does in the worship of the major Earth shrine. For both the contributions to sacrifices and the apportionment of them are sometimes calculated on a homestead basis.

But I am here concerned not with the functions of the dwelling group as such but rather with its spatial and kinship structure. It is to the first of these that I now wish to turn, for analysis of the internal disposition of the dwelling group is the analysis of the spatial distribution of the groups we have been discussing; they are all contained within the homestead. The dwelling group represents a point in a merging series of territorial groups. It is subdivided into rooms and sets of rooms and itself forms part of a more inclusive territorial organization.

As in other societies the buildings reflect the composition of the dwelling group. But the fit is much closer in a society where the houses are built from mud than when they are made from more permanent materials such as stone. On account of the heavy rains repair work is an annual affair. And if a room is not required because of the death or departure of its occupant, it will soon fall into ruins. The plan of the homestead acts therefore as a fairly exact map of the social relations of the members of the dwelling group and it is with this plan that I shall first be concerned.

The LoDagaba homestead is very similar to that of the LoWiili. Its external wall of swish is six feet or more high and encloses a series of rooms, most of which are covered with a flat roof of mud laid on wooden rafters. Each party wall projects through the roof, which therefore provides a complete plan of the homestead. It is on the roof that the men spend most of their spare time during the day, while the women work mainly in the rooms below. At night the occupants usually sleep on the roof of their own room as the breeze is cooler there and keeps off the mosquitoes and other insects.

The simplest type of homestead, illustrated in Fig. 1, is that which contains an elementary or polygamous family. It consists of an open patio (*davra*) where most of the cooking is done. Leading from the courtyard runs the long room (*tʃaara*) in which the central granary is built; it is here that the women gather when performing their daily tasks. In the long room are the entrances to the women's rooms (*diu*, pl. *dir*). Standing on the edge of the compound, with a door leading into the courtyard, there is sometimes a grass-roofed hut for the use of the husband or of his adolescent sons. This type of room is always peripheral to the main compound and not built until after the rest of the house has been finished. It is, I believe, of comparatively recent introduction. Apart from this, the husband has no room of his own, unless as a widower he builds a hut on the roof.

As the household grows by the addition of wives, so the rooms increase in number. Each wife has to have one room to herself when she has children to

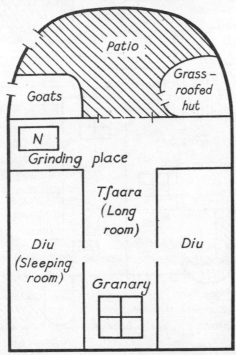

Fig. 1. A dwelling of the simplest type, occupied by an elementary family. Diagonal lines indicate unroofed walled area. Broken line indicates line of posts supporting roof.

look after. Each cooking unit has to have its own kitchen (*miiru diu* or *koro diu*). When the sons of these women grow up and marry and have children, their wives too will have rooms of their own. Thus there will be a gradual expansion outwards from the original room belonging to the mother. An open patio will be added to give outside cooking facilities and to provide a urinal. Further rooms, including possibly a grass-roofed unit for the son, are built and the mother's old room becomes the central long room of the new set.

A set of rooms is a duplicate of the simple homestead. It has its own long room, granary, sleeping quarters, fowl room and usually but not invariably its own open courtyard. The byre where the cattle are kept is not duplicated; this has ritual significance for the unity of the dwelling group, for it is here that all the ancestor shrines are kept. But otherwise the set forming a simple homestead is repeated as the dwelling group grows.

Cooking groups tend to occupy independent sets. This is not to say that when two women cease to cook together a new set emerges immediately. What happens is that each woman will have her own inside kitchen where she

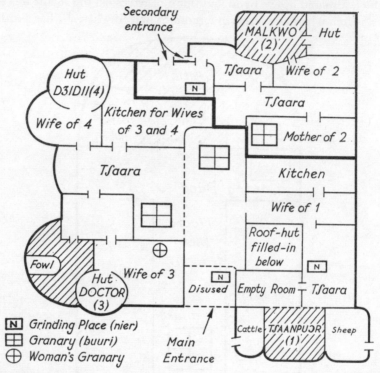

Fig. 2. The compound of Tʃaanpuor, a dwelling of the complex type. Diagonal lines indicate unroofed walled area. Broken lines indicate line of posts supporting roof. Thick line indicates boundary of enclosed apartment with separate entrance. Quarters of adult married males are given in capitals.

can cook and store her food. It is only when the sons grow up and take wives of their own that a new set of rooms will be created. This often happens in the following way. When adult sons are working with their father, the unit of production both needs and obtains a larger harvest and another central granary is required to store the grain. The new granary will be built not in the main long room like the first but in the senior wife's room where it will eventually form the nucleus of a new set of rooms. Separate sets are therefore the spatial correlate of units of production rather than of consumption. Every unit of food production must, of necessity, have its own set as it requires its own main granary. In a farming group of fathers and sons it is the sons of the senior wife who are the first to be ousted. They will take over the granary in their mother's room or if necessary build a new one, leaving the original main granary to be inherited by the youngest son of all, the one, that is, who has continued to farm with the father.

The fission of units of food preparation requires a reorganization of the spatial arrangements in the homestead, the establishment of different cooking places and storage rooms. The growth of the unit of food production leads to internal differentiation and the establishment of different sets of rooms. All units of food production have their own sets. These spatial rearrangements are stages leading to the fission of dwelling groups. But there is another, intermediary, stage. The increased social distance between farming groups is demonstrated by the decrease in communication between them. The specific material form this takes is the closing of the entrance from the original long room to the new set. This was originally the entrance to the woman's room. When the latter became a subsidiary long room it was the main entrance to the new set from the remainder of the house. Finally the door is walled up so that direct access is impossible.

The blocking up of the communicating door between different sets is paralleled by the appearance of separate entrances to the dwelling itself. This is different from the LoWiili homestead which has no direct entrance from ground level. The only opening from outside leads into the cattle byre from which there is no access to the rest of the house. One has to climb up a ladder on the outside wall leading to the roof and then descend into whatever patio one wishes to go. The LoDagaba also have external ladders by which visitors enter the homestead. But in addition the LoDagaba house has also at least one entrance on the ground floor and it is through this that the women carry their pots of water and the young children move to and fro between the compound and the shade tree which stands nearby.

Apart from the main entrance (*dondɔr kpɛ̃ɛ̃*), there may also be other entrances known as *dondɔr blɛ*, a phrase which is also used for a subdivision of a unilineal descent group, usually one other than the speaker's. In this latter context it has a pejorative significance, not only because it indicates a descent group which has broken away from the original stock but also because it is the word employed to designate the child of an unmarried girl. These secondary entrances often seem to have been made accidentally. What appears to have happened is that a patio wall has fallen down or was not completed at the time the house was built. When the occupants are asked about this they sometimes reply 'We'll build that up after the rains.' In fact, it is very doubtful whether they will actually do so. For wherever one set of rooms is shut off from another, both have their own independent entrances from the outside, even though this may be only a gap in the patio wall. That is to say, they do not rely upon ascent to roof and descent into the patio by a ladder, as the LoWiili do.

These separate entrances, approximately equal to the number of enclosed sets of rooms, are yet a further index of the approaching fission of the dwelling group.

A sketch of a typical example of an expanded household is shown in Fig. 2. There are four adult males in the house: 1. Tʃaanpuor, 2. Malkwo, 3. Doctor, 4. Dʒidii. The spatial arrangements indicate the social relations of the occupants. The three long rooms show there are three sets and the three main granaries that there are three farming units. 3 and 4 plainly belong to one unit of production as their wives have the same indoor kitchen and therefore form part of one unit of consumption. This implies that their wives do not both have children who have been weaned.

Further deductions are possible on the basis of this sketch. It is clear that as 3 and 4 constitute one farming unit, the genealogical relationship between them is likely to be closer than between any other pair of male occupants. They will, moreover, be more closely related to 1 than to 2 because they share an entrance with the former and not with the latter.

The genealogy below shows the relationships between the occupants of the homestead.

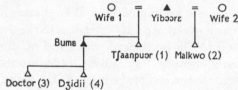

Malkwo (2) is a younger paternal half-brother of Tʃaanpuor (1) and of the dead father of the two other occupants. The greater social distance between 1 and 2, as compared with 1 and the father of 3 and 4 is demonstrated by the existence of a separate entrance to 2's set of rooms, whereas both 1 and 3–4 enter by the original long room. Consequently the connecting door between these sets has remained open.

Now that I have described the internal differentiation of dwelling groups, the process of accretion and the connection with the units of reproduction and production, I want to turn to the numerical and kinship structure of the group.

First, the numerical strengths of the compound. The thirty compounds in Tom Zendaagõ had an average of 17·63 persons a compound, the range being from 4 to 46. This average was made up as follows:

Men	Women	Children
3·70	5·03	8·90

The comparative figure for the LoWiili sample was 16·45 distributed in the following way:

Men	Women	Children
4	5	7·45

The 1948 census for the whole of the LoWiili gives the figure as 17·4.

Thus although the farming groups among the LoDagaba are smaller than the LoWiili, the compounds are if anything larger. This would appear to support my interpretation of the data, although I would in any case be hesitant of taking the differential size of dwelling groups as indicative of greater or lesser conflict within the agnatically based domestic groups.

Let me now turn to the relationship structure of dwelling groups. As might be assumed from the previous figures, the span of agnates among the two groups is very similar. I measure the span of agnates by the number of generations in the unilineal genealogy from the junior members to their common ascendant. For example, where the common ascendant is a father, this is shown as one generation. The following table gives the comparable data.

Table 7. *The span of agnates in dwelling groups*

Span of agnates	Generation					Common lineage only	Common clan only	Total
	1	2	3	4	5			
LoWiili								
No. of groups	6	8	7	2	1	0	1	25
Percentage	24	32	28	8	4	0	4	100
LoDagaba								
No. of groups	5	10	9	0	0	2	2	28
Percentage	18	36	31·5	0	0	7·25	7·25	100

Although there is no difference between the two communities in the agnatic component of dwelling groups, there is in the non-agnatic element. The main category of these, apart from wives, are sisters' children, and the numbers of these living in the above compounds at the time of the census is shown in Table 8.

Table 8. *Sisters' children living with matrilateral kin*

		Sisters	Sisters' children				Total
			Infants	Under 14	Over 14		
					male	female	
LoWiili	Temporary	3	4	1	0	0	8
	Permanent	2	0	5	5*	1	13
LoDagaba	Temporary	4	6	0	0	0	10
	Permanent	0	0	0	0	0	0

* Plus 3 wives and 2 infants. Another sister and her daughter lived in a homestead on their own.

Among the LoDagaba compounds there were six sisters' children. These were the children of four sisters, three of whom, together with their five children, maintained they were on temporary visits to their kin. But it is significant that in the case of two out of three of those on temporary visits, as well as in the case of the other sister who was on a lengthy stay following a quarrel with her husband, that the woman's widowed mother was still living in her natal homestead. Indeed of the seven widowed mothers living in these homesteads, three of them had married daughters and their young children staying with them at the time of the census. I mention this fact, inadequately documented as it is, because a daughter's return visits to her paternal home after her marriage are often analysed solely in terms of the pull of the agnatic lineage against the marriage tie, the latter gradually becoming firmer as the marriage endures. But this is only one aspect of the gradual decrease in visits to the paternal home. My data suggest that there would be a significant difference in the length and frequency of visits before and after the mother's death, and that this would be greater when the mothers are widowed than when they are married. The insistence on a daughter's continued membership of her descent group after marriage has tended to obscure the strength of maternal filiation in women and the matricentral nature of a girl's adolescence.

The only sisters' children resident with agnates among the LoDagaba are these infants who are in the care of their mothers. Among the twenty-eight LoWiili compounds there were in all three sisters with two young children on temporary visits. One sister's daughter of two years had been taken there to be looked after by her maternal grandmother because her mother had just died. In another compound, a sister's daughter of ten years of age was on a short visit to the house into which she was expected to marry. In addition two sisters with six adult children were living permanently with their male agnates.

On the basis of these figures there appears to be a greater tendency for an adult to live with his mother's brother in the community in which all property is vested in the *patrilineal* descent group rather than in the community in which wealth is inherited in the *uterine* line. This I believe is indicative of the different relationships between a man and his mother's brother when this relationship is characterized by the holder-heir situation. In the LoDagaba sample, there were no cases of an adult living with his mother's brothers, that is with the man whose wealth he is to inherit. This would appear to be because of the conflict between the two persons involved and the difficulties of sons and sister's sons being in the same compound. Among the LoWiili the relationship is less liable to tension and is indeed more typical of a patrilineal society in general. A sister's son can live at ease in his mother's brother's compound as there is no implicit tension over the property. It is significant, however, that in the two LoWiili cases where this did occur the mother was still alive. The sister's sons were living with their matrilateral kin on the strength of the mother's position as a member of the patrilineage. It is likely that both groups would build their own dwellings after their mother's death. While she is alive sibling ties hold the dwelling group together. I would stress that this mediation of the mother in the relationships of a man with his mother's brother is a matter of the membership of property-holding descent groups rather than a question of the 'extension of sentiment' from the mother to her brother. This can be seen by reference to the LoDagaba where, as far as co-residence is concerned, sibling solidarity is not strong enough to over-come the fissiparous forces created by the matrilineal inheritance of wealth.

To summarize the data presented in this section, LoDagaba and LoWiili dwelling groups are essentially similar both in numbers and in composition in respect of the agnates which together with their wives form its core. It is with regard to the non-agnatic inhabitants—that is, the children of sisters—that differences occur. In the LoDagaba there were no adult sisters' children living with their mother's brothers; in the LoWiili sample, there were six, five males and one female. This difference was related to the greater tension ex-isting between a man and his maternal uncle in a society in which wealth is inherited from him at his death.

CONCLUSION

In this paper I have examined the organization of domestic groups among the LoDagaba in terms of the three-generational cycle of development. I main-tained that the analysis of this aspect of social life was inhibited by the assumption that the central focus of this process was necessarily the 'nuclear family' as visualized by Malinowski, Murdock and other writers. Among the LoDagaba the 'nuclear family' is the nucleus neither in the productive, nor in the reproductive process. In the process of reproduction, the smallest unit is the conjugal pair, or, from another point of view, the minimal lineage. In the process of production, which was the one mainly considered here, different groups emerged at the various stages of the cycle of production, distribution, preparation, and consumption.

In this community, agriculture is largely a male activity and the basic farming unit is a group of agnatically related males, a paternal (father-son) or fraternal (full-brother) unit. Dependent for agricultural produce on this male agnatic core, is a group of women and children who contribute their labour toward weeding and harvesting. But the basic unit in the process of distri-bution, preparation, and consumption consists of a mother and her young children, and the adult males are in this context seen as attached to the matrifocal group. This alignment is clearly related not only to the particular social division of labour, but also to the female's biological functions of child care which are extended into later life by various social institutions.

This system of organizing domestic units influences the cycle of their development. For instance, when fission occurs between the agnatically related males, it initially takes place in terms of the matrifiliation of the persons concerned. And this process is reflected in the reasons given for the segmentation, that is, the state of subdivision, of more inclusive groups, şuch as higher-order lineage segments.

In order to see clearly the operation of the process of cyclical fission among the LoDagaba, a comparison was made with the nearby LoWiili who, although they had a similar system of dual clanship, inherited all property patrilineally. There were three main differences between the two communities. As far as food production was concerned, the farming group was found to be smaller among the LoDagaba than among the LoWiili. In the distribution of food, LoDagaba wives had a greater proportion of the total crop placed under their control after the harvest. And, thirdly, analysis of the composition of dwelling groups showed that the incidence of residence in the mother's brother's homestead was greater in the group where no property was inherited from him, that is, among the LoWiili. All three of these differences were related to the differences in the system of property relations. The smaller farming groups among the LoDagaba resulted from the fact that persons who were not uterine kin split earlier in order to avoid the situation whereby, in the event of the death of one member, the wealth which they had accumulated jointly would be inherited by a member of another group. The different systems of food distribution and the different types of granary were also related to the fact that the LoDagaba place greater quantities of grain under the control of their women to avoid the situation in which the heir could claim the whole of the food supplies and leave the widows and their children destitute. The lower incidence of residence in the mother's brother's homestead among the LoDagaba was held to indicate the greater tension between mother's brother and sister's son in communities where this relationship is characterized by the holder-heir situation. The corollary of this proposition is that in fully-fledged dual descent societies like the LoDagaba, there is a decrease in father-son tension, despite the apparent contradiction of earlier fission of farming groups. For although the father is a main socializing agent and male role model with respect to his children, as in all societies where the conjugal pair is co-residential, this relationship no longer bears the additional brunt of the entire holder-heir situation.

This paper forms part of a general comparison of the social systems of these two communities and it is difficult to elucidate the general points arising from this 'controlled experiment' without reference to other aspects dealt with elsewhere. Broadly speaking, these general points might be said to arise from certain suggestions made by Radcliffe-Brown in his paper on *Patrilineal and Matrilineal Succession* (1950) concerning the importance, in relation to the existence of unilineal descent groups, of the method of transmitting relatively exclusive rights, particularly those over objects of property, women, roles and offices. Although the method of transmitting these rights is intimately connected with the structure of unilineal descent groups, there is no one-to-one correlation of systems of inheritance with systems of descent. The case of the LoDagaba illustrates this point. And from an examination of the instance where this discrepancy exists, it would appear that the significant variable for cross-cultural analysis of nuclear kinship relations is not 'linearity' in itself but rather the method of transmitting these relatively exclusive rights within and between generations.

APPENDIX

Table 9. *The distribution of wives of adult men among the LoDagaba*

Single men			Married men, number of wives				
Not married							
Under 20	Cripples, lepers and blind*	Widowers and deserted†	1	2	3	4	5
5	4	4	45	17	4	1	0
Percentage of sample							
LoDagaba			56·25	21·5	5	1·25	0
LoWiili			61	17	6	0	2
Tallensi			46	20·5	4·1	4·8	0·7
Percentage of married men							
LoDagaba			67·2	25·2	6	1·5	0
LoWiili			71	20	7	0	2
Tallensi			60·4	27	5·4	6·3	0·9

* One other blind man is married and has two wives.
† There were two widowers, very old men, and two younger men whose wives were temporarily away visiting their agnatic kin.

Only wives actually living with husbands were included in the table, otherwise the problem would have been too greatly complicated by terminological difficulties. The LoWiili and LoDagaba figures are very close, particularly when it is considered that there are no Christians among the former and some 25% among the latter. This is, I think, explained by the fact that at this stage of mission activity it is the poor men who become Christians.

NOTES

[1] In the Tallensi books, he speaks of one group as the 'domestic family'. This is defined as a 'segmentary jural and ceremonial formation' and is characterized in terms of the homestead as having its own gateway.

[2] Nadel distinguishes between sections and segments (1951: 178).

[3] In his table of average farm areas Hinds shows the LoDagaa as having no bush farms. This is in the main correct for the LoWiili but it certainly is not true of the LoDagaba. His classification of farms into 'periodic fallow' and 'bush' depends only upon the extent of growth of the shrubs and trees in the fallow period. The existence of such a continuum may well have affected Hinds' categorization of his material.

[4] The higher proportion of fathers farming with sons among the LoDagaba requires some comment as it might appear to contradict my general thesis. If we

include the one case of a LoDagaba father farming independently of all his sons, this gives a total of ten LoDagaba with adult sons as against six among the LoWiili, seven if the illegitimate son of the sister is included, as he is locally. I have explained that I do not think the age distributions varied significantly. This difference may be accounted for by a slightly earlier age of marriage among the LoDagaba, though it is more likely to be due to the fact that I excluded the category 'youths' when adding up the LoWiili figures.

[5] This homestead was not included in the LoDagaba sample.

[6] Not salt, as this is a foreign product which has to be purchased in the market.

[7] The *kazaari* is distinguished from two other categories of grain which are also set on one side at this time. First, there is the *kaper*, the remnants left from last year's harvest at the time the granary is cleared out and fumigated to make room for the new crop. This is usually taken to the market to be sold. Sometimes a husband may sell it cheaply to his wife. The other category is *kakube*, the grains which are left on the roof when the harvest, which is first laid out there to dry, has been stored away. This can only be used for preparing beer for ritual purposes, that is, for funerals and for certain sacrifices. There is one additional category. This consists of the best heads which are kept aside for next year's seed.

[8] It should be added that it is only for the evening meal that this arrangement obtains. If a man wants food in the middle of the day it is the wife in whose room he is sleeping at the time whom he asks to prepare it. The sleeping arrangements are closely intertwined with the cooking and in this particular respect the distribution of sexual services is reciprocal to the preparation of food.

[9] Elsewhere I heard of cases where the father eats with all his children, though this would seem to be a new practice. In order to even out the shares the father might make the child of one mother eat from the same bowl as the child of another.

[10] I found no such cases among the LoWiili. But there the women spent less time in agricultural activities. In the first place, the acreage farmed was less, in the second, the fields were nearer to hand, and in the third, farming parties only expected to be fed on their third and last appearance in the season.

[11] The Bekuone patriclan have a ritual prohibition on their wives looking into the main granary. I was told of one man who had divorced his wife for having disobeyed this rule.

[12] I use the phrase 'first order matrisegment' to distinguish these domestic groups from more inclusive lineage segments which may also be differentiated on the basis of maternal filiation.

[13] I use the word homestead to designate a dwelling the constituent parts of which are contiguous with one another, preferring to retain the term compound for dwellings where the constituent 'rooms' are already separated one from another.

REFERENCES CITED

Barnes, J. A. 1955, 'Seven Types of Segmentation', *The Rhodes-Livingstone Journal*, no. 17.

Durkheim, E. 1893, trans. 1947, *The Division of Labour*, Paris.

Firth, R. 1936, *We, The Tikopia*, London.

Fortes, M. 1945, *The Dynamics of Clanship Among the Tallensi*, London.

—— 1949(a), *The Web of Kinship Among the Tallensi*, London.

—— 1949(b), 'Time and Social Structure' in *Social Structure: Studies Presented to A. R. Radcliffe-Brown*, Oxford.

Fortes, M. 1957, 'Malinowski and the Study of Kinship', in *Man and Culture*, ed. R. Firth, London.

Fortes, M. and Evans-Pritchard, E. E. 1940, *African Political Systems*, London.

Goody, J. R. 1954, 'The Ritual Institutions of the LoWiili and the LoDagaba', unpublished Ph.D. Thesis, Cambridge University.

—— 1956, *The Sociology of the LoWiili*, London.

—— 1957, Fields of Social Control Among the LoDagaba', *Journal of the Royal Anthropological Institute*.

Hinds, J. H. 1951, 'Agricultural Survey of the Wa-Lawra District', *Bull. of the Dept. of Agriculture*, Gold Coast.

Malinowski, B. 1930, 'Kinship', article in *Man*, London.

Murdock, G. P. 1949, *Social Structure*, New York.

Nadel, S. F. 1951, *The Foundations of Social Anthropology*, London.

Radcliffe-Brown, A. R. 1929, 'A Further Note on Ambrym', article in *Man*, London.

—— 1950, *Structure and Function in Primitive Societies*, London.

Rattray, R. S. 1927, *Religion and Art in Ashanti*, Oxford.

HOUSEHOLD VIABILITY AMONG THE PASTORAL FULANI

By DERRICK J. STENNING

In this paper, 'family development' refers to cyclical changes in the size and composition of viable domestic groupings based upon the family. These are changes brought about by the birth, marriage, and death of family members. They involve not merely changes in family constitution, but affect, and are affected by, the relation between the family and its means of subsistence, which, as a domestic unit, it manages, exploits and consumes in close co-residence, continuous co-operation, and commensality. Such a domestic unit is viable when the labour it can provide is suitable for the exploitation of its means of subsistence, while the latter is adequate for the support of the members of the domestic unit.

In this paper, the principles of these relations are explored in the context of the social organization of the Pastoral Fulani, who are the principal cattle-owning nomads of the western Sudan. Particular reference is made to the tribe known as *Woɗaaɓe* (sing. *Boɗaaɗo*), who inhabit the Fune, Damaturu, and Gujba Districts in the west of Bornu Emirate in north-eastern Nigeria.[1]

In Pastoral Fulani society, the domestic unit is based upon the simple family (a man, his wife and their offspring) and its extension in the compound family (a man, his several wives and their offspring). Ownership of herds is vested in the male heads of such families, whose members carry out the essential tasks connected with cattle husbandry, forming the nucleus of a household living in a distinct homestead.

Changes occur in the size and composition of simple and compound families. A simple family commences as a legal union of husband and wife in marriage. This union is devoted to the procreation of legitimate children, their care during infancy, their socialization, and their material support until sexually mature. This unequivocal process of expansion comes to an end when the first child, particularly the first male child, marries and reproduces, setting up a similar simple family. From now on, the original family is in a state of dissolution. This may be concealed, however, by the birth of further children to it when the full reproductive span of spouses, particularly the male spouse, is utilized in polygynous unions. Complete dissolution—excluding the eventuality of death or divorce of spouses—occurs when all their offspring have married.

HOUSEHOLD VIABILITY AMONG THE PASTORAL FULANI

The relationship between transfers of cattle, first marriage, and the inauguration of distinct households and homesteads suggests that the simple or compound family is the optimum viable domestic unit in Pastoral Fulani society. However, viability of the simple or compound family is adversely affected by a number of factors. These are of three types: regular seasonal variations in the demands of the pastoral economy; irregular natural hazards; and the formal properties of the simple or compound family itself in relation to its means of subsistence throughout the period of its growth and dissolution.

In response to certain aspects of these adverse factors, domestic groupings based upon the agnatic joint family emerge. However, these are of short duration, breaking up again into their constituent simple or compound families. Other aspects of the non-viability of the simple or compound family are met by forms of co-operation which do not involve the formation of wider domestic units. Most of these, like the formation of agnatic joint family domestic units, are based upon the agnatic relationship of household heads. The functions of the agnatic lineage, and to a lesser extent the clan, are thus mainly those concerned with promoting the viability of their constituent simple or compound family households as domestic units.

The formal development of the simple family begins by definition when children are born to the spouses. But in Pastoral Fulani society this must be regarded as only one stage—although a crucial one—in the formation of a domestic unit based upon the family. Anterior events must be considered, and it is convenient to describe the whole formal development of the family in terms of a male who is to be a family head, a householder, and a herdowner.

In these terms, the process begins when an infant boy is given a name, seven days after birth. He now becomes a person as this is understood for males by Pastoral Fulani; he has cattle. In the presence of his male agnates, his father sets aside for him a calf or two which are the nucleus of his future herd.

The next important occasion is at his circumcision, at between seven and ten years of age. He now becomes a herdboy, competent to take cattle to daily grazing. He is given some useful token of this service—a leather apron, a gourd water bottle, or a set of Koranic charms. He is taken into his father's cattle corral and 'shown his beasts', and further calves are again allocated to him, again in the presence of witnesses who are his male agnates. He has the nucleus of a herd, and every herd must have its dairywoman, the wife of its owner. He is therefore betrothed to an infant girl.

The next stage, still a preliminary to the formation of a family, household and homestead, is the induction of the betrothed girl into the homestead of her future husband's father. This takes place when she is known by the latter to have begun menstruation, and is therefore believed capable of childbirth. The couple sleep together in the open at the boy's post on the perimeter of the cattle corral. In other respects—participation in ceremonial and in work—the couple have the status of unmarried youth and maiden. The youth still carries out his duties of herdsman to his father's herd, including those cattle set aside for him. The girl becomes, as it were, a daughter of her husband's father's household, and works under the supervision of one of his wives, properly the mother of her husband. The youth and girl continue to participate in ceremonials proper to those who are not herdowners or wives, and act mainly as instructors of song and dance to younger participants.

This ambiguous period ends with the conception of the couple's first child. When the girl's pregnancy is evident to her husband's father's wife, she is removed to her own father's household. There she undergoes a period of seclusion during her pregnancy, and remains for three wet seasons—two to two-and-a-half years—after which she returns to her husband.

On this occasion it is not a pair of spouses taking up residence, but a family, and all the appurtenances of family life—a distinct homestead and a distinct herd—are to be provided.

Compared with the clusters of circular, thatched mud huts which constitute in some form or other the hamlets and villages of most of the sedentary populations of the western Sudan, the homesteads, and camps, of the Pastoral Fulani seem haphazard and rudimentary. In the wet season even a large camp blends with the bush, and in the dry season it is possible to pass within a few yards of a homestead without realizing it is there, unless its herd is present. Household equipment is limited to the amount which may be carried on the head or on pack animals, and shelter must be made of whatever tree foliage the district has to offer.

In spite of the rudimentary and impermanent nature of the homestead, it exhibits an important degree of formality and uniformity.

Pastoral Fulani homesteads always face west.[2] In all but overnight camps a curved back fence of branches cut from nearby trees is put up to ensure a measure of privacy, keep out hyena, and deflect the course of stampeding cattle frightened by their nightly visits in the wet season.

Immediately in front of the back fence are set the beds of the homestead, the essential poles, slats, and coverlets of which are transported when camp is moved. Over the bed is erected a structure similar to it which forms a platform on which are placed the household utensils. In the wet season this platform is elaborated to form a shelter. Its components are, again, transportable. Alongside, behind, or in front of the bed-shelters there may be other ancillary shelters put up for specific purposes. These are low, beehive huts of springy boughs covered with bark matting, or tall shelters of heavier leafy boughs. These shelters do not contain beds made with poles, but a rough couch made of bundled grass and bark mats.

In front of the bed shelters there is a domestic hearth, consisting of three stones or parts of white-ant nests as a support for a cooking pot, supplemented perhaps by an iron tripod.

Near these shelters and in front of them is kept household stock other than the herd of cattle—a horse or donkey hobbled and tethered to a forked stake, and a small flock of sheep or goats sheltered in a fold made of stout branches.

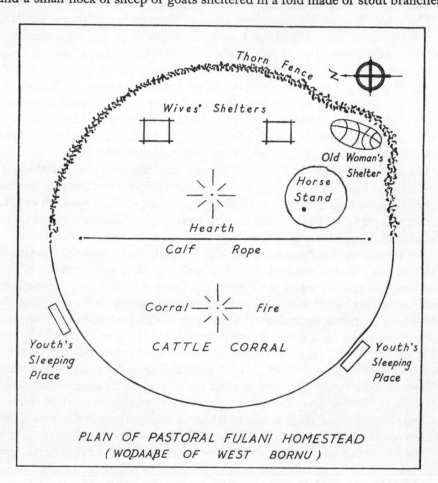

PLAN OF PASTORAL FULANI HOMESTEAD
(WODAA̧BE OF WEST BORNU)

In front of this group of shelters is staked down a long two-stranded leather rope, to which the calves of the household herd are tethered whenever the herd is present, to prevent their suckling except when their dams are to be milked. In front again of the calf-rope is the cattle corral. This is usually just a circular patch of earth trampled by the beasts' hooves, but where wood is plentiful a corral fence may be put up. Round the corral under convenient bushes or trees there may be rough beds of the type to be found in the ancillary shelters. In the centre of the cattle corral there is a smudge fire round which the cattle gather in the early morning and in the evening when they return from pasture. The fire is always lit, even in the rain, on the return of the cattle, and extinguished after they have gone out to pasture the next morning. The ritual importance of the corral fire is attested in the myths recounting the circumstances under which the first Fulani obtained cattle.

The whole homestead, consisting of one or more bed-shelters, ancillary shelters on occasion, calf-rope and cattle corral, is the basic residential unit of which all Pastoral Fulani local units, in the form of camps, are built up. The general shape of a camp is that of a rank of homesteads facing west, with their calf-ropes and bed-shelters in the same straight line from north to south. Larger camps are formed with the addition of other such ranks of homesteads pitched to the east and west, but never due east and west, of the first rank. There is no exact term for such camps in their residential aspect; the most general term for a camp is merely the plural of 'homestead'.

The essentials of the homestead—the bed, the domestic utensils, the calf-rope and the herd—are ceremonially brought together when the wife returns to her husband with their first-born child. There is a striking symmetry in the homestead plan, which canalizes the day-to-day life of family members, and the sources from which household property accrue to the new family.

The wife's natal family provide her with the objects of a wife and dairymaid. First among these is her bed. The bed poles are cut and trimmed by her brothers, and stained red by her sisters. The grass mats and bark coverlets are made or bought by her mother. The latter is also responsible for providing the ceremonial domestic equipment of a dairymaid—calabashes, dippers, churns, spoons and so on, lashed together with leather thonging in a traditional way. The site of the wife's domestic quarters lies alongside and to the north of her husband's father's homestead; it is cleared and fenced by the latter's sons. The husband's father also provides the pack-ox, with its harness, on which the new wife's bed and domestic equipment are transported when camp is moved. That part of the homestead which is predominantly the wife's, and which is essentially feminine in character, is thus complete.

The masculine component of the new homestead is the cattle corra., and this comes into being when the husband lights his corral fire in front of his wife's shelter.

One component of the new homestead remains—the calf rope. This is made by the husband's father and brothers, who peg it in position when the new homestead is being set up. The calf rope divides and yet unites the two halves of the homestead.

The wife's side of the homestead is to be given over exclusively to the day-to-day execution of women's tasks. A wife will maintain her own property. She will prepare milk and butter for sale, and milk and cereal foods for home consumption. Infants of both sexes and unmarried daughters will eat with her; they may be joined by the household head's son's childless wife, his daughter home for her first pregnancy, or his widowed mother. No female will eat outside this domestic area, and no male, other than infants, will eat inside it.

On the husband's side of the calf rope are the cattle, the main interest and preoccupation of the men, in their corral. Here, at dawn and dusk before milking time, the male household head will be joined, for an appraisal of the herd's condition, by his herdboy sons. The latter will sleep at the corral perimeter. The household head and his sons will eat in order of age seniority at a point on the western side of the corral. Here those males who are in camp during the day will work, mostly at making the many varieties of rope required in connection with livestock. Here they will also spend the evening round a fire, their circle often augmented by a ring of cattle who have 'come to be admired'.

As the family grows, the everyday activity of its members will be canalized by the division of the homestead into its male and female sections. In a general sense, entry into the corral is forbidden to females, entry into the wife's section is forbidden to males.

There are two important exceptions to this rule. A husband will cross the calf rope to enter his wife's shelter, to lie with her, to beget children. A wife will cross the calf rope to milk cattle whose calves have been released to them by her husband. The congress of husband and wife in the wife's shelter will concern children; the congress of husband and wife in the corral will concern calves.

Calves are identified with children, particularly male children, in many overt ways. A first-born son at his mother's back wears a ceremonial collar which is a replica of the halter which tethers calves to the calf rope. Boys below herding age are expected to take care of calves close to the homestead during the day while the herd is at pasture. A group of boys or youths in a dance who are age mates are called by the term for a calf rope.

But the calves at their calf rope play an important part in the ceremony at which the homestead is inaugurated. The homestead is prepared, the corral fire lit, but the new herd can be constituted in only one way. While the herd of the father of the new household head is away at pasture, the calves of his son are tethered to the calf rope of the new homestead. When the herd returns, cows allocated to the son find their calves elsewhere, and it is to the new homestead they go. The attachment, to the new herd, of cows which have no calves at the time of its constitution, must await calving, for which they are tethered in the corral of the new homestead. Bulls are separated by being tethered there for a few days and are then loosed in the evening when the herd returns from pasture, until finally they run exclusively with the new herd. But it is the transfer of calves which makes possible the orderly formation of the new herd. If the first-born is a son, there is a calf or two in the newly constituted herd whose progeny will form the nucleus of a new herd at the third human generation.

The subsequent development of the simple family is in effect the marital history of the male household head, which takes place against the background of the expansion of the herd which he owns. Normally, sons and daughters are added to the simple family. It may be expanded into a compound family by the addition of wives up to the legal Muslim maximum of four, and, again, children may be added to these matricentral components. Divorce may take place, but normally the children born to a man stay with him, or are claimed by him when they are no longer infants, at the age of seven to ten. All these developments are crucial in considerations of the viability of the simple or compound family household.

But for the moment it is convenient to turn to the usages surrounding the dissolution of a family in the period of decline in the marital history of its head. Sons have been born to him and allocated cattle, which, in the normal course of events, have had their increase. His sons have shared the duties of herding and watering the whole herd, and, as their power and skill as herds- men have increased, the cattle allocated to them have also increased. At the point at which, in addition, they have demonstrated their own powers of procreation, their allocations of cattle have been turned over to them on the formation of their homesteads and households. The herdsmen's skill has now been devoted to their own cattle, which in turn provide their dependants with subsistence. They have ceased to be sons, but have themselves become husbands and fathers.

But while these developments have been taking place, the father's personal power and skill as a herdsman and as a begetter have been waning. Although polygynous marriages and the children resulting from them may temporarily conceal the fact, he is steadily losing dependants as they get married. Allocations of cattle have depleted his herd. A man's last unmarried son herds his father's cattle, but on his marriage they all become his own.

Although distorted by the incidence of divorce and paternal rights to children, the case of a mother is parallel in Pastoral Fulani eyes. When her homestead was set up she was given decorated calabashes, which were never used but proudly displayed on ceremonial occasions, symbolizing her milking rights in virtue of her status as a mother. On the birth of daughters, decorated calabashes were given her by her mother and sisters. But as her children married her responsibilities for feeding them ended, while her reproductive faculties declined. She gave her own decorated calabashes to her daughters until finally, on the marriage of her last daughter, her stock of decorated calabashes and her responsibilities as a mother, housewife and dairywoman came to an end.

Sons and daughters married, the couple no longer constitute a family. The wife has no calabashes, because she has no milking rights; her husband has no herd in which she might milk. They no longer live in a homestead of their own. The shelter and the calf rope are abandoned. The couple take up residence as dependants, each with his or her eldest son, even where this involves living in the same homestead. The old woman lives in one of the ancillary beehive shelters behind her sons' wives' shelters. The old man sleeps in the open in front of his eldest son's corral. The old woman may be of use in caring for her son's infants, who may sleep in her shelter. But an old man is regarded as of little use. He may help in making rope, but he has no voice in planning the movements of the cattle of the household. Old people in this situation spend their last days on the periphery of the homestead, on the male and female sides respectively. This is where men and women are buried. They sleep, as it were, over their own graves, for they are already socially dead.

This description has for the moment gone rough-shod over many palpable demographic, ecological, and economic factors. But it permits the salient ideal feature of family development among the Pastoral Fulani to be presented. This is that the social interpretation of the passage of the generations in a domestic context is one which provides for the formation of viable simple or compound families constituting the basis of households, living in separate homesteads and subsisting upon distinct herds. This interpretation includes the important notion that this process should take place without prejudicing the viability of the parental household. It may be summarily concluded that the optimum viable domestic unit is the simple or compound family.

Given this identification of the simple or compound family with its herd, the limiting conditions of viability may be outlined. The Fulani described here as 'Pastoral' are part of that section of the Fulani population who are not farmers, fishers or traders as well as cattle owners, but whose subsistence and wealth derive solely from the herds they possess.

A herd is a distinct group of cattle consisting of at least one stock bull, and a complement of cows, heifers and calves, together with pack oxen. It is distinct in that it normally reproduces itself by in-breeding and line-breeding, spends the daytime period of grazing apart from other similar herds, is watered separately, and spends the night in a corral reserved or constructed for it and marked by its special smudge fire. As already stated, the corral is part of the homestead of the male herdowner, who is responsible for its day-to-day management and who directs the necessary activities of the simple or compound family subsisting on it.

Given circumstances in which cattle are the sole basis of subsistence for such a household, meat does not form a regular or staple diet and animals are not sold frequently, since this represents a draw on the capital stock of the herd. Killings are confined to male beasts, or where possible, sick, maimed or barren animals. Such killings occur only on important ceremonial occasions. Sellings take place only when an overriding need for cash occurs; for example to buy corn in the dry season, or to raise tax. The family, then, lives on milk; unlike some of the pastoralists to be found in East Africa, Fulani do not drink cattle blood or make blood foods. Either milk or milk products must be drunk and eaten *ad nauseam*, or milk must be sold or exchanged in favour of other foods. Thus the limiting factor in the subsistence of a given family upon its herd lies in the milk output of the latter. There is a minimum size, composition and (since lactation is a condition of reproduction) fertility of a herd in relation to the subsistence requirements of the family associated with it.

The herd has here been considered as supporting the family dependent upon it. But there is a sense in which the family supports the herd. Fulani cattle are not natural groups of wild animals followed and exploited intermittently by human groups. Fulani herds are in a particular way domesticated, and this domestication entails a degree of special organization in the families dependent upon them. The diverse pastoral skills of herdowners and their sons are directed towards the achievement or maintenance of a state in which the family can subsist on the herd's milk and the cereal foods for which it is exchanged. Desirable pastures have to be sought and cattle led to them. Water supplies have to be arranged and cattle watered regularly. Diseases and accidents of many kinds have to be avoided, or their results treated. Cattle have to be protected from the attacks of wild beasts, and thefts must be prevented. Pack oxen must be trained, and the birth of calves assisted.

The preoccupation of the wives of herdowners, helped by their daughters, is the control, by careful milking, of the supply of milk available to calves and humans, and the sale of butter-milk, butter and sour milk on as favourable terms as possible in such markets in cereal producing areas as are made available to them. The Pastoral Fulani family is a herdowning and milk selling enterprise.

Given this strict division of labour and a herd of a given size, a family must attain a certain size commensurate with its responsibilities towards its herd, and a composition which ensures that these are efficiently carried out by appropriate members of the family.

When the size and increase of the herd is adequate for the subsistence of the family, and the size and composition of the family are suitable for the control and deployment of the herd, then family and herd may be said to be in equilibrium, and the unit as a whole is viable. But both the human social unit and the means of subsistence associated with it are breeding concurrently, each within well-defined though different limits of fertility; the fertility of each affecting, indirectly, the fertility of the other. Thus in the life-history of a family and its herd, expressed as the lifetime of a male household head, the state of equilibrium and viability is not constantly fulfilled. There arises a whole range of temporary, partial, or potential disequilibria which require resolution.

However complicated the incidence of non-viability, it can be seen to have two main aspects. In one range of cases, non-viability is a condition in which there are not enough humans to cope with the cattle assigned to them. In another there are not enough reproductive cattle to feed the humans associated with them. Finally, and more rarely, junctures in the history of family and herd arise in which both these conditions occur simultaneously.

Loss of viability occurs in three main contexts. First, it may be due to regular seasonal variations in the demands of the pastoral economy. Secondly, it may be due to irregular natural hazards. Thirdly, it may be due to the formal properties of the simple or compound family itself in relation to its means of subsistence, throughout the period of its growth and dissolution. The last context is the main concern of this paper, but it would not be doing justice to crucial conditions in the social life of Pastoral Fulani if the first and second were not discussed. Indeed, a discussion of the regular seasonal changes and irregular natural hazards does much to justify, in ecological and economic terms, the assertion that the simple or domestic family is the optimum domestic unit.

The Pastoral Fulani inhabit the savannah zone of the western and part of the eastern Sudan. The savannah zone of the western Sudan constitutes a transition area between the Guinea zone to the south, and the Sahara desert to the north. From south to north it is characterized by a diminution of the mean annual rainfall, and progressive deterioration of the vegetation from tall tropical forest to sparse thorn scrub. Perennial tsetse fly infestation in the Guinea zone, and continuous shortage of pasture and water in the desert, preclude cattle-keeping in those zones, while the dominant characteristics of the savannah render it, in general, favourable for this form of exploitation.

But the savannah zone is not immutable as a cattle-keeping zone, and with the seasonal interplay of the wet south-west monsoon from the Atlantic and the dry north-east monsoon from the Sahara, its characteristics change. In the wet season the southerly part of the savannah zone tends to take on the characteristics of the neighbouring Guinea zone and becomes fly-infested. In the dry season, the northern part of the zone becomes practically desert as standing water is evaporated and herbage dried by the sun.

These conditions enjoin upon the Pastoral Fulani of the savannah zone a movement north in the wet season and south in the dry season. This transhumance has much variation in impetus depending upon local conditions of pastoral and sedentary population density and yearly variations in the onset, intensity and duration of the rains. In west Bornu, where low sedentary population density means that movement of pastoralists is practically un-impeded by farmland, the Woɗaaɓe move uniformly, every two or three days, in accordance with the phases of the moon.

But it is not merely movement which is imposed by the changing seasons upon Pastoral Fulani if their herds are to be maintained. The wet season is marked by a congregation of family households to form camps, while at the height of the dry season much smaller groups of family households, single households, and even matricentral components of compound families camp on their own. In the wet season greater concentrations of cattle are possible since there is adequate pasture and water; and greater concentrations of humans dependent upon them follow. In the dry season, the grazing area of a herd must be much larger, and households are consequently dispersed. But this is not the complete answer to the general problem of seasonal dispersal and congregation. It is likely that the total area of savannah zone land denied to Pastoral Fulani in the dry season by pasture and water shortages is considerably less than that denied them in the wet by tsetse fly and growing crops.

As these seasonal changes unfold, the family labour devoted to the herd and the sustenance obtained from it undergo significant changes. In the cool wet season, herding is at its easiest, although made disagreeable by the rain. Cattle drink at pools close to the homesteads, pasture close at hand, and may return replete to the vicinity of the camp in the early afternoon. A woman regards her wet season work as easy compared with that of the dry. Markets are probably equally available in both seasons, and for the arduous work of obtaining domestic water in the dry season is substituted the enjoyable task of preparing for wet season feasts. Milk yields are higher in the wet season, partly because of the increased number of lactations, partly because of good fodder; there is a considerable surplus for use in feasts.

These conditions deteriorate steadily till the height of the dry season. Now, daily grazing takes place over wider tracts in which grass cover is far from uniform, and in which herdboys are expected to move into surrounding bush to find stands of more profitable herbage. Meanwhile, standing water may be non-existent, and improvement of existing water-holes, as well as the back-breaking task of watering cattle, has to be carried out. In addition, reconnaissance of potential pasture farther afield, across tracts of burnt-out country on horseback, is the task of a good husbandman. The principal addition to the work of women and girls is the task of obtaining domestic water. All these tasks place a strain on the labour resources of the family, and are of a kind which not only require men, women, boys and girls to work harder, but also demand the labour of more hands, particularly so far as herding and watering are concerned.

Complementary to these changes in the contribution of the family to the herd are the changes in the contribution of the cattle to the family. The natural breeding cycle of herds is such that calving takes place mainly in the early wet season or wet season proper. However, serving of heifers and cows is not controlled by herdowners as stock bulls run with the herd at all seasons. Milk supply is curtailed by the lower proportions of lactations occurring in the dry season, and also by the lower yield of such lactations as do occur as a result of poor fodder and high temperature.

Changes from wet to dry season are thus likely to affect the viability of a family household and its herd, both by a relative shortage of humans due to the amount and type of labour required and by a relative shortage of cattle due to the decrease in the number and yield of lactations. It is dry season conditions which bring these changes about, and no family remaining viable in the dry season is likely to find itself non-viable in the wet season.

The second context in which changes in viability occur is that of the irregular natural hazards, of accident or disease resulting in the death of cattle. The death of single beasts in the herd rarely affects the household viability, except for the death of the stock bull, which temporarily renders all the cows and heifers worthless. But bovine disease has striking effects. Non-infectious diseases, the most important of which is trypanosomiasis, may cause severe shortages of cattle in individual herds, but since in the normal course of events the location and duration of tsetse infestation are well known to Fulani, widespread incidence of trypanosomiasis is not common. Infectious or contagious diseases present a different picture. Formerly rinderpest was the most important of these, but has been largely eradicated by European veterinary measures. Nowadays, bovine pleuropneumonia, the Fulani treatment of which is normally prohibited by the Administration without any offer of an alternative, is the most deadly. Here, isolation at as great a distance as possible of small groups of cattle, with the early slaughter of infected beasts, is a measure accepted by Pastoral Fulani and encouraged by the Administration. The disease runs its course in whichever herd is affected, and few beasts recover. Where isolation is impracticable, or where the disease breaks out at a period of maximum concentration or close movement, as in the wet or early wet seasons, contagious or infectious diseases may strip of their cattle whole local communities of Pastoral Fulani.

It may be said that these extreme eventualities have little to do with the normal process of Pastoral Fulani grouping in relation to the means of subsistence. Nevertheless the eagerness with which Pastoral Fulani concur with at least the spirit of the Administration's policies regarding bovine diseases, and the horror with which the details of (for example) the great rinderpest epidemic of 1897 are recounted, are evidence to the contrary Bovine disease is a possibility of which the herdowner has constantly to be aware. Together with the seasonal variations in amount and quality of pasture and water, the possibility of disease is a factor conditioning the salient features of human and herd organization—mobility, and ability to disperse into the smallest possible units consistent with subsistence. Finally, a consideration of seasonal variations and irregular hazards serves to show that viability is not merely an automatic aspect of the development of families and herds in the course of the lifetime of the household head.

It remains to consider the loss or lack of viability in the family household engendered by its own formal properties throughout the period of its growth and dissolution.

It is necessary first to establish the minimum viable unit, in terms of the minimum herd which will support the minimum number of persons whose labour is necessary to it. It was found that Woɗaaɓe informants had a clear idea of these minima. First, they stated that there should be one prime stock bull to every twenty-five head of cattle. (Although informants did not suggest this, herd output surveys for Bornu red longhorn herds lead to the supposition that not less than half such a herd should consist of bearing cows and heifers.)

Such a herd requires the services of one dairywoman and one herdsman; and by dint of unremitting labour, a man and his wife might, and have been known to, support such a herd all the year round. However, this entails their removal from many fields of social and economic activity.

This minimum herd can, however, support more than two humans, and it is on this supposition that Woɗaaɓe base a more realistic assessment of the minimum labour force required. To fill his position in society effectively, and also to exploit his means of subsistence to the full, no herdowner can devote every day to herding cattle. Other tasks have to be carried out, and other relationships maintained, if a herd of any size is to be deployed to the greatest advantage. The principal ancillary task is the making of the many types of rope continuously used, and worn out, as fetters, halters, harness and so on. The principle set of relationships are those in which intelligence concerning the natural and political conditions in the tracts of land over which herds are continuously moved, is obtained. A man herding cattle sees only the pasture to which he has been committed; a vaster range of potential grazing land and water resources is open to him, the value of which he must continually assess in conference with those who currently know it. It is in the market places, where Pastoral Fulani from the surrounding country, and sedentary non-Fulani from distant villages, foregather, that informed opinions are amassed and sifted in endless discussion for the herdowners' future advantage. Thus for the proper care of even the minimum herd its owner requires the services of a herdboy. A boy can herd cattle and carry out the tactics of herd deployment; but the decisions of strategy, which to Pastoral Fulani are more important, lie with the herdowner.

A wife, too, is only partially fulfilling her responsibilities when she is concerned solely with work, such as milking and marketing, which is directly concerned with the herd. Her responsibilities include those of childbearing and the care of infants, and these are inimical to her other duties. Thus unmarried daughters market milk when their mothers are pregnant, or take care of infants while their mothers go to market. The wider duties of both husband and wife are concerned with the future independence of the family unit, in the assurance of conditions in which the herd will flourish, or in the provision of future herdboys and milkmaids. Thus the more realistic estimate of the size and composition of the family in relation to the minimum herd is a man and his wife, and their son and daughter.

In the ideal situation, these conditions are already partially fulfilled at the inception of the family. A husband and wife acquire their separate homestead and their herd on the condition of having a child. However, at the outset of its history, a family is bound to be non-viable in one, if not both senses. It may commence with an effective minimum herd, but even if the first-born were twins—a rare and, in Pastoral Fulani eyes, most happy circumstance—it could not commence with an effective minimum family. The achievement of this condition takes at least five or six years from the installation of the family in its homestead. This is the period in which a boy will grow to the herding age of seven to nine years. Thus in spite of the creation of a separate homestead and the establishment of a herd over which its owner has full rights of deployment and disposal the family undergoes at its inception a period of non-viability, in respect of shortage of humans, and perhaps of cattle as well.

Subsequent developments in the internal constitution of the family are connected with its viability as a domestic unit. Additional children may accrue to the simple family; new matricentral components may be added by polygynous marriage. Wives leave the family by divorce; they may take their infant children with them for good, or these children may return to their father when they are no longer infants. Both wives and children may be lost to the family through death.

The social institutions regulating these fluctuations—in so far as they are able to do so—are those connected with polygyny, divorce and the affiliation of children. These are to be reviewed against the marital contract implicit in the procedure and symbolism of the establishment of the homestead and herd by first marriage. This is one in which the expectations of a husband in his wife are that she should bear him children, particularly boys, the labour force and inheritors of his herd; while the expectations of a wife are that the husband should maintain sufficient cattle for herself and her children. The principal result of the unrestricted application of such a rule would be that men with the most cattle, and therefore the most fertile herds, would be able to take to wife the most fertile women, and more of them. Similarly, men might be expected to divorce their wives when they did not bear children, women to divorce their husbands when they were provided with insufficient cattle to milk.

It may be claimed that to a large extent the data (of which only a summary can be given here) support such an interpretation. The institutional evidence with regard to women's reproductive performance in relation to marital history must first be outlined. The tensions inherent in the period of first residence of a betrothed girl with her husband, which is dominated by the interest of the husband's father in an early conception, must first be recalled. Unless brought to an end by early pregnancy, this unstable period is concluded by a breakdown of the betrothal. The establishment of a homestead and herd is traditionally contingent upon the birth of a wife's first child, and the procedure of first marriage includes this event by definition.

Although miscarriages and premature deaths of her children are not *prima facie* grounds for divorce of a woman by her husband, there is evidence to show that during the course of her marital history unduly lengthy intervals between births of her children may bring divorce upon her. This is difficult to substantiate from women's childbearing histories, but it has the support of institutional evidence. Male sterility, which may, in fact, be the cause of such intervals, is not recognized by Pastoral Fulani men and may result in the divorce of a woman by her husband. More important here are the rules concerning the custody of children after the divorce of their parents. The custody of boys who have reached herding age and thus have acquired a firm interest in the paternal herd, and of girls for whom betrothal arrangements have been made, is vested in the husband of their mother. But the custody of infants still in the care of their mother is dependent upon the circumstances of the suit of divorce. In brief, either spouse may repudiate the other, and divorce is permitted, easy and frequent, although there are important variations caused by the uneven acceptance of the jurisdiction of Muslim tribunals. Unless the spouse who is repudiated acquiesces, the spouse making the repudiation forfeits rights to infants in the care of their mother at the time of the conjugal separation which precedes divorce; and in theory at least to any child born during the wife's *edda*[3] which concludes it. These rules favour the maintenance of marriages in which there are infants, for the spouse initiating divorce must be prepared to lose either the present custody or the future services of such infants when grown up. For a man they also maintain the firm attachment of herdboys to the paternal herd. For a woman they may secure her old age, for however many marriages she enters, she has a right to be supported by her eldest son when she has passed childbearing age.

The conditions which render unstable a woman's marriage before she has borne children, and during gaps in her childbearing history, also make the onset of menopause a crucial period in her marital career. Whether the onset of menopause in a wife is itself grounds for divorce by her husband depends upon whether she has infants still dependent upon her, whether her husband is polygamously married, and whether her co-wives have infants dependent on them. In the absence of other grounds for divorce, a woman keeps her bed and domestic belongings, and thus her rights to milk, while she has infants to support. When this is no longer the case, and all her sons and daughters have respectively received their patrimonies or are betrothed, she is eligible for conjugal separation or divorce. Where the matricentral component of which she is the head represented the last responsibility of her husband, his family, household, homestead and herd are dissolved in the way described above. In such a case divorce proceedings do not have to be instituted, the process merely consisting of conjugal separation. It should be noted in passing that, just as it is most fitting that a man's first-born should be a boy, so should his last child. Where this is not the case, a son's marriage is delayed until his elder sister marries.

Where the husband of a woman who has reached the menopause has other wives, conjugal separation may occur and she may become dependent on her eldest son. But she may as an alternative be divorced, particularly where her husband wishes to undertake another marriage within the Muslim legal maximum. Finally it should be noted that the sanctions applicable to widow inheritance marriage (which will be discussed below) operate most effectively in the case of young widows, not those who are nearing the end of their childbearing period.

These practices are associated with others which confirm the interpretation of the marital contract set forward here. If the likelihood of divorce of a woman by her husband is greatest at the beginning and end of the menarche and in intervals in which she does not bear children, the fate of a barren woman is one of continual insecurity, unless she can marry where her domestic virtues are of more importance than her reproductive capabilities. A barren wife's best hope is in the fertility of her co-wives, for a woman who is childless but of equable disposition and a hard worker may, in certain circumstances, be a good foil to a co-wife whose main role is that of mother. There are alternative courses for barren women. Some, unable to find a domestic situation of the type just described, enter a succession of marriages which take them further from the preferred endogamous loci of marriage into 'strange' clans of Pastoral Fulani; into the ranks of semi-sedentary Fulani, or sedentary non-Fulani villagers. Others move, more quickly, into prostitution in the towns.

A second consistent feature of marital histories which is associated with the foregoing conditions is that there is a growing disparity in age between a man and his successive wives.

These conditions demonstrate the institutional factors supporting the contention that the principal expectation of a Pastoral Fulani man in his wife is that she bear him children. The complementary expectation, of a wife in her husband, which is now examined, is that he maintain a herd sufficient for the support of herself and her children.

A herd may prove or promise to be insufficient for a wife's needs in two ways, each of which may occasion the recrimination of a wife and make divorce on these grounds more likely. First, the herd itself, or its milk output, may be reduced, and secondly, the household dependent upon it may be increased by a further matricentral component, so that a wife has at her disposal relatively less milk.

Actual reduction of herds by disease, loss or sale, is regarded by Pastoral Fulani women with varying degrees of contempt for the cattle owners. There are ceremonial occasions on which oblique references in extempore songs may be made by girls and women to the shame brought upon them by disease in the herds. This contrasts strongly with men's attitudes which are usually expressed in a way which suggests that a herdowner takes all reasonable precautions to avoid disease. The only true cattle medicine is good husbandry and disease is the work of Allah.

Reduction of herds by sale is not normally contemplated without pressing need for cash, and a good husband consults at least his senior wife when cash has to be raised. Women, rather than men, encourage side ventures in small stock such as sheep and goats, which can be sold when cash is needed without depletion of the herd from which their main subsistence is derived.

Conversely, women do not approve efforts of their husbands to better themselves politically when this involves presents to chiefs not in the pastoral community in whose gift a certain title may lie. Nor do they support sales of stock to purchase a horse, saddlery, a sword and gowns, which are necessary if a man is to make his mark in this way, unless the reproductive part of the herd remains untouched.

Women will also disapprove of the sudden migrations which are usually made for political motives, and the occurrence of such a migration is accompanied in marital histories and genealogies by a number of divorces of men by their wives. But normally, so long as they have access to markets and domestic water supplies, Pastoral Fulani wives support the seasonal movements of cattle.

A corollary of the opposition of women to courses of action which decrease the herd, and therefore, actually or potentially, its milk output, is that in the dry season, when milk output is unavoidably low, the conjugal separation which constitutes or leads to divorce is more likely to take place. At the height of the dry season, when temperatures are at their highest, food at its scarcest, watering and herding of cattle at its most arduous, and family units most dispersed, there is little doubt that the possibility of internal friction in the family is more pronounced than in the wet season. Fortunately, the tasks of this time of the year disperse even more than usual the personnel of the family, so that friction is automatically minimized. Nevertheless it is well recognized by Woɗaaɓe that the difficulties of the dry season exacerbate any latent friction between husband and wife, and that wives are more likely to run away at this season. It is also easier to do so without detection, owing to the dispersal of kinsfolk and the pastoral preoccupations of the season. In the wet season, when kinsfolk are congregated, an absconding wife will be quickly discovered. Moreover, this is a time when domestic friction is lost in the sense of more general unity which the ceremonies then carried out engender, and in the air of plenty and well-being fostered by easy pasturage and ample food.

The second way in which the herd upon which a wife depends for her supply of milk is decreased is a relative one, caused by the increase of the total household dependent upon it. The principal way in which this occurs is by an addition to the household head's establishment of a further wife, and, immediately or subsequently, of her children. In contrast to the reasons for divorce arising from absolute reductions in the herd, in which the interests of the husband and wife are at issue, those springing from relative reduction of the herd are based upon the antipathy of co-wives.

A wife for whom a herd was constituted, that is, a first wife by betrothal marriage, always has superior rights to milk in it over her husband's wives of inferior categories. It is said that this wife apportions rights to milk to junior wives. Although the wife for whom the herd is set up is normally a man's only wife at that time, it may happen that a husband takes another while she is away at her father's home for the birth of her first child. If such a wife remains in the household when the first wife returns, the latter's superior status is asserted in a custom in which the junior wife hides her face in her headcloth, and suffers a mock beating at the hands of the senior wife. The junior wife does not set up her bed until the senior wife is installed, and she does so to the south, or right-hand side, of the female domestic area.

This brief ceremony expresses the rivalry which is a consistent feature of the relation between co-wives. The divergence of interests of co-wives is demonstrated in three interconnected ways—in rivalry for the sexual attentions of the household head, in the achievement of greater influence in the household through the birth of children, and in the outward signs of this, the number of cattle allotted for milking. The rivalry of co-wives thus extends in some measure to their male children, the half-siblings who acquire cattle by allotment and inheritance on the basis of the differential rights of their mothers to milk specific cattle in the total paternal herd.

Rivalry for the sexual attentions of the household head is kept at a minimum by a strict rota which by its association with obligations of feeding the household head is uninterrupted during menstruation and extends well into pregnancy. Nevertheless quarrels leading to divorce do occur ostensibly on this score.

The rivalry of co-wives concerning the birth of children is seen primarily in the rules connected with parturition, conspicuous amongst which is that enjoining the mother to deliver all children but her first herself, without the assistance of her co-wives, who are normally the women nearest at hand. The operation of the rules concerning the custody of infants in divorce does not fail to produce anxiety in wives whose childbearing has temporarily or permanently ceased and the resultant tension lies between co-wives rather than between husband and wife.

Finally, a monogamous wife is loth to welcome a second wife to the household unless her domestic duties in milking and handling calves as well as taking care of children grow too great for her and any unmarried daughters she may have, owing to the size of the herd. In seeking divorce, Pastoral Fulani women may not merely be escaping from a domestic situation they regard as intolerable, but seeking one which represents an advancement for them in terms of the number of cattle they may have at their disposal for milking.

It can be seen from this brief description of the institutions of divorce and polygyny that in Pastoral Fulani society women's marital histories are highly variable. They are liable to be divorced if they bear insufficient or no children. They may initiate divorce if, when they have borne children, their husband's herd proves inadequate for their needs. They are liable either to initiate divorce or be divorced if they are living in a compound family, and the herd proves inadequate for the maintenance of the whole unit. The full extent of this instability of her marriage bond is found at the beginning and end of a woman's childbearing period, but one or all of these circumstances may recur during her marital history.

It follows that the matricentral group of genetrix and children or mater and children in Pastoral Fulani society is also unstable. It is true that a mother cannot be separated from her infant children, who go with her in conjugal separation, and it is also true that the conjugal tie is firmest when there are infant children in the family. But as children reach the age of betrothal, they may be claimed by a former husband. Only at the end of a woman's reproductive life does the maternal tie reassert itself and then only between mother and son, when she claims her right to his support. A female's life may thus be spent in a number of domestic families headed by different herd-owning males. As an infant she may live in the homestead of her pater cum genitor; or of her genitor only. As a girl who has been betrothed she lives in the homestead of her pater, who may also be her genitor. She then takes up residence for the first part of her marital life in her husband's father's homestead, returning to the homestead of her own father, not of her mother, for the birth of her first child. Her subsequent marital history during her reproductive life may be spent in one, often a succession, of husband's homesteads. Her declining years are spent with a son, or close agnatic kinsman of junior generation. One point deserves special recognition here. At stages or intervals when a female is a potential wife—that is to say, when she is a betrothed girl, or a divorced or widowed woman in her *edda*—she remains with her pater or close agnatic kinsman until marriage or remarriage.

The resultant picture of a Pastoral Fulani woman's career is one of continual dependence, in some sense or other, upon males, whether pater or genitor, husband, male agnatic kinsman, or son. During the reproductive period, and indeed when it is over, the marital stability of this career is contingent upon her reproductive performance. The birth and survival of one son will secure a woman in her old age, but not necessarily keep her in one homestead all her married life. But a full and evenly spaced family is likely on the evidence to do so; and it is in these conditions that a woman transcends the status of dependant, wields considerable influence with her husband, and may even, as Pastoral Fulani say, 'be greater than a husband' and seek a more prosperous herdowner as a spouse.

Consider by contrast the career of a male. Endowed almost at birth with the means of his future subsistence; incorporated at an early age into a tightly organized partnership with father or brothers and trained by constant precept and practice in the tasks of the pastoral regime until he emerges as an independent householder, the Pastoral Fulani male stands, it appears, in a more secure position. He lives in principle in two homesteads during his life—that of his father, or guardian, and his own.

This apparent security is not wholly the case, for a man's household suffers changes in composition as a result of factors for which he bears responsibility. For just as a woman's marital stability depends upon her own fertility, so does that of a man depend upon the fertility of his herd. A man's own fertility is, characteristically, not believed to enter into the question. Male sterility is not recognized; there must be a woman, somewhere, by whom a man can have children. Social institutions support this; a man may acquire a family through the clandestine adulterous relations of his wife, or a wife may bring children from a former marriage.

The fertility of the herd depends, first, upon the skill and diligence of the herdowner in securing for it the optimum conditions of reproduction within the limits of the habitat. A number of maxims and ceremonies, and much of Fulani notions of prestige, support this interpretation of the direct responsibility borne by the herdowner for the fertility of his herd. To this extent the responsibility of a Pastoral Fulani woman for her own fertility, and that of a man for the fertility of his herd, are comparable. Where a woman's fertility is inadequate she moves on, in divorce, to another man, and perhaps right outside the Pastoral Fulani community. But much can be done to prevent a herd's numbers sinking below the effective minimum, or, when they have done, to regain it, and to adjust the amount of labour available to the herd. Herd-owners are members of agnatic descent groups whose members combine for greater or longer periods or in different ways to initiate, maintain, or reinstate families and herds in a state of viability. The part played by agnatic kinsmen in the various contexts and states of non-viability will now be discussed.

The first of these is in the seasonal variations. In the wet season, the congregation of households is based upon the agnatic kinship of male house-hold heads. These gatherings have little to do with economic co-operation as such, since at this time of the year the constituent households are experiencing the least difficulty in either the amount of labour required for the herds, or the provision of subsistence from them. The wet season gatherings constitute rather a demonstration of the solidarity of the agnatic descent group in which actual economic co-operation may be expected by its members; and the wet season rituals and ceremonies express this. In addition, relationships are entered into which tend to guarantee the viability of the constituent families in the future.

It has been seen that with the advent of the dry season, the wet season congregations disperse under the pressure of natural conditions. But the dry season conditions may make a given family household non-viable in respect of shortage of labour or of shortage of cattle. Thus as the dry season wears on the demands of pastoral co-operation grow, against a more general need for dispersal.

Where the shortage is one of cattle, the necessary dispersal of families is allowed to go unhindered, and households are not merged. This shortage is met by a series of loans of cattle, including both trained and untrained oxen for transport work, and stock bulls. The principle reason for such loans in the dry season is, however, the maintenance of the milk supply of a given household. Cows or heifers with calf at foot are used for this, and transferred readily between the herds of agnatic kinsmen. Cows in calf are not transferred, for it is the task of the herdowner, who bears direct responsibility for the fertility of his herd, to assist in the delivery of its calves. It should be noted that among the Woɗaaɓe calves born in bush without the assistance of the herdowner are sold after weaning. Similarly cows and heifers are not placed in an agnatic kinsman's herd to be served and eventually calve. This takes place, but it belongs to a different series, not of loans but of exchanges, between herdowners of different clans. The genetic function of such exchanges is to break the train of line-breeding and in-breeding in the herd. The social function is to secure extra clan ties. Loans between agnatic kinsmen, however, are made with no consideration of cash or kind. The obligation both to loan animals to a needy kinsman, and to return them, rests on moral sanctions, applicable to the clan, which among the Woɗaaɓe are only recently challenged by the Muslim courts. Loans of this kind for milk supply do not extend beyond the weaning of the calf in question; loans of pack animals seldom extend into a second dry season.

Shortage of labour in the dry season can be met in various ways, only some of which involve merging of households. The shortages of labour apparent in the context of the seasonal variations are those of dairymaids and herdboys. Shortages of girls usually arise where a wife is in an advanced stage of pregnancy, or has an unweaned child; and the difficulties of such a situation become most obvious in the dry season. In compound families a measure of co-operation is expected of co-wives, so that when a wife is prohibited from milking in virtue of her pregnancy, her co-wife milks and markets for both. Daughters, too, are interchangeable between the matricentral components of compound family households, assisting in marketing and, in particular, sharing the task of getting water for the whole household.

In the simple family household the shortage of female labour is met by the wife's 'borrowing' an unmarried sister, or sister's daughter, to help in her domestic work.

Where in the dry season the tasks of herding and watering become too arduous or various for the herdboys of a family household, the difficulty is met in two ways. Daughters and even wives may be required to help with herding or more usually with watering. But this is an extreme solution and one which appears most usually to be brought about by conditions necessitating extreme dispersal at the height of the dry season.

Normally, where through dry season conditions there are not enough herdboys, two family households merge for the purpose of herding cattle. The homesteads are pitched side by side, and each herd spends the night in its own corral in which a corral fire is lit. But the herdboys of the two households are put on a common rota for herding, and look after both herds at once in the bush, for the herds do not merge when such temporary co-operation is carried out. The herds are watered separately, girls or women perhaps being brought in to help. The herds are milked separately by their respective dairywomen, and it should be noted that there may be milch cows borrowed from agnatic kinsmen in either herd. The herds are merged only for surveillance while grazing, and one form of co-operation does not rule out another.

The loss of viability due to irregular natural hazards is met again by the co-operation of herdowners of the same agnatic descent group. Where non-contagious diseases affect only parts of herds, deficiencies are met by loans of stock on the pattern described above. Where a whole herd is stricken, and the herdowner cannot recoup by loans, he may do so by outright gifts from agnatic kinsmen and clansmen. Nowadays when slaughtering is enforced in outbreaks of infectious and contagious diseases, cash compensation is paid by the Administration. Among the Woɗaaɓe the head of a herdowner's agnatic lineage group acts as his agent for the receipt of compensation. But although compensated, herdowners in many groups of Woɗaaɓe are still reluctant to build up their herds again by purchases of stock in the open market. Indeed such purchases of unknown cattle are rightly believed to further the spread of virulent and lethal diseases like bovine pleuropneumonia. The agnatic kinsmen of such herdowners supply them with cattle in the traditional way, in return for a share in the compensation money, agreed between the giver of the stock, its recipient and the head of the agnatic lineage group. Such a persistence of the reciprocal rights and duties of agnatic kinsmen in emergencies of this kind is advantageous to all parties. The herd of the unfortunate cattle owner is re-established with cattle of the most desirable breed, whose history is known. The givers of cattle acquire a cash return which can be set against future expenses such as cattle tax. Both parties are saved the inconvenience of buying or selling in the open market, and avoid cash losses involved in the services of middlemen. The sole intermediary is the head of the agnatic descent group, and the proportion of the compensation which he receives is spent on objects such as a gown or a turban, a sword or horse trappings, which confirm his status and ultimately redound to the prestige of his followers.

When the dispersal of households is not enough to alleviate the worst effects of an epidemic, this reciprocity perforce breaks down. It is now that a herdowner may recoup on the basis of extra-clan ties arising from cattle exchanges, or on extra-clan affinal relations. But these are weaker both in number and in the material relief they bring than the co-operation of agnatic kinsmen. Although widespread epidemics thus involve the dispersal of agnatic descent groups, and their incorporation, by families or individuals, into other such groups they may also mean the removal of families from the pastoral community either temporarily or permanently.

In the context of the seasonal variations and irregular natural hazards, the agnatic descent group and the clan are agencies for the re-establishment of the viability of their constituent families. This function emerges primarily when non-viability is caused by shortages of cattle. Indeed the ability of an agnatic descent group to act in this way is contingent upon the dispersal of its constituent families. Only by endowing household heads with full responsibility for the fertility of their herds and full authority for their deployment is it possible to succour any member of the agnatic lineage group whose family cannot maintain its viability.

It remains to consider the part played by agnatic kinship of household heads in the formal process of development of the family from its foundation to its dissolution. In the case of regular seasonal changes and irregular natural hazards, the agnatic lineage group has been seen to further the maintenance or re-establishment of viability of simple or compound family households. In the present case its function lies primarily in effecting the inception of family households, and secondarily in promoting their early viability.

It has been shown that it is at the inception of a family that both its requirements in cattle and in humans are most likely to be unsatisfied. It has also been mentioned that marriage is virilocal, male residence patrilocal and inheritance patrilineal. Thus on the formation of a man's domestic unit, his new establishment lies, typically, alongside that of his father. The relation of father and son at this period is one in which the son is independent of his father in some respects, dependent upon him in others. The degree of dependence will be seen to lie with the state of viability of the father's family.

On the formation of his domestic unit, a newly married son has, in theory, a certain independence. His wife may prepare food for him, which he may eat, if he chooses, in his own homestead. He may now sell cattle and may provide beasts for slaughter at ceremonies, the first of which is likely to be the name-giving of his second child. He may now be responsible for raising his own share of cattle tax. He has a voice in camp councils, as a herdowner, and may give not only evidence, like a herdboy, but express opinions concerning it. He may move away from his father, and other agnatic kinsmen if he so desires, in the dry season.

In practice it is found that newly married sons stay with their fathers, often all the year round, eating in their father's homestead, being assisted by him in raising tax or ceremonial obligations, and siding firmly with him in camp councils. That this is so, in spite of a degree of theoretical independence, is due to two factors. First, the control of cattle loans and gifts remains with a man's father until his social or physical death. Secondly, the state of non-viability in the sense of shortage of both humans and cattle experienced almost inevitably by a herdowner's domestic unit on its inception, in relation to the viability of the parental domestic unit, keeps the two households together, for at least the period it takes to train a herdboy in the filial family.

Although a newly married man might decrease his herd, by sale or slaughter, as soon as it is established, and is bound to ensure its increase by careful deployment, the right to maintain it in adversity by loan or gift does not lie with him while his father is alive and in control of a herd of his own. For a son in this situation to ask for loans of cattle among his agnatic kinsmen of the same or senior generations is to repudiate all the efforts of his father as herdsman and begetter. This may take place, but in repudiating his father a man repudiates his agnatic descent group; the outward sign of such disaffection is not to return to the common wet-season camp. It should be noted that a young married man, who may have ranged farther afield than his father in seasonal movements, is still at liberty to arrange exchanges of cattle with herdowners of other clans.

Given this proviso, that a father controls accession of cattle by loan or gift to his son's herd, there is considerable variation in the degree of independence of the paternal and filial family households. This variation depends upon the state of viability of the parental family—that is to say, the extent to which it is unnecessary for a father to call into action the resources of the agnatic descent group for the benefit of his son. A few examples will make this clear.

Immediate separation for all except the period of the wet-season ceremonies, and maximum independence of the two households, is found to occur at the upper end of the scale of prosperity in cattle, and in the parental household best endowed with sons. A rich herdowner has been able, at the time of the inception of his eldest son's household, to support a number or succession of wives, and to exercise rights of residence over their children. At the same time his allocation of cattle to his son has been such that the latter's herd emerges immediately as an effective herd. In a case of this sort, the eldest son of each matricentral component, except the last, of the parental household, might well acquire the services of his younger full-brother or brothers, and be able to move freely in part if not all of the dry season.

A more normal case is one in which a newly married son withdraws from herding, while the herds of father and son are herded on a rota common to the newly married man's younger brothers. Here the parental and filial households remain together until the son's herd is effective, and he has a herdboy son to look after it.

A further case at the opposite extreme is where the father has only two sons. In this case the newly married son is unable to assume completely the status of herdowner since he is occasionally required to herd cattle. Here it is not so clear which of the two households is dependent upon the other. In a final case, that of a last son, dependence is passed over to the father, who as described above takes up residence with his son, his herd, family and homestead having been dissolved.

In all cases there is no question of postponement of marriage of a son by his father. This contingency is eliminated on the one hand by the prolongation of the life of the father as pater or genitor, or both, in successive or simultaneous polygynous marriages. On the other it is obviated by the fact that the men who are concerned to marry off their daughters to each others' sons are precisely that group in which co-operation in loaning cattle is enjoined. Household heads of an agnatic lineage group or set of agnatic descent groups dispose of their daughters in marriage to men with whose fathers they enter into reciprocal rights of pastoral co-operation in lending cattle.

But given marriage of both men and women at the earliest possible time consistent with notions of reproductive capacity, it is certain that from the beginning a newly married son partakes of his father's status as a herdowner. At one end of the scale he becomes head of a unit consisting of himself, his family and his unmarried brothers, which is pastorally, though neither ceremonially nor in emergency, independent. At the other end of the scale, lack of cattle gives his theoretical independence little meaning, while his father's shortage of labour restricts both father and son in those activities associated with herd ownership.

Thus, in summary, the inevitable period of non-viability which falls upon a newly established household is met by merging for certain purposes the households of father and son. This association is one of dependence of the son upon the father, due to the latter's control of loans and gifts, and of the greater possibility of co-operation between agnatic kinsmen of the father's own generation than between those of the generation of his son. The minimum period of this association is five or six years, although in certain circumstances which are rare in west Bornu today an immediate separation of father and son is possible. During the dry season the separation of parental and filial families is the criterion of their mutual viability. Their camping together in the wet season is an expression of the importance of this close agnatic tie.

The management of the inevitable period of non-viability in a newly formed household has been discussed on the assumption that a father sees all his son's marriages. But the formation of all a man's sons' homesteads and herds, much less their attainment of viability, is rare among the Woɗaaɓe. It is more likely that physical death of the latter precedes the point of his social death, so that he leaves behind him unmarried children, fertile wives, and un-allocated cattle. A man dies in two conditions relevant to the present issue: leaving sons none of whom has married and established a family and herd, or leaving some sons married and some unmarried.

In the case where none of the sons has married, it is a principle that the dead man's brother or patrilateral parallel cousin, usually a junior, shall act as the guardian of the dead man's children and supervise their betrothals. Under the witness of the family heads of the agnatic descent group, and with the mediation of its leader, he becomes the custodian of the dead man's herd, and turns over their portions to the dead man's sons as they marry. He should inherit at least one of the dead man's widows, particularly when of child-bearing age. He should devote the increase of the unallocated balance of the dead man's herd to the support and provision at marriage of any of the children he may beget by her. The inherited widow's milking rights extend over this unallocated balance. In a case of this kind, the dead man's brother or close agnatic kinsman of the same generation is as nearly as possible his substitute.

But where a family head dies leaving some sons married with families, homesteads and herds, and others without, this substitution in the collateral lines is not practised. Although the dead man's brothers or patrilateral parallel cousins may now act as adjudicators or witnesses in the settlement of his affairs, the guardianship of minors and the custody of the herd falls to the dead man's eldest son. A brother or cousin may marry the dead man's widow, and it is thought proper that this should happen, but in this case she and her offspring must be provided for out of his own herd, unaugmented by any of the dead man's cattle.

Thus although among the Woɗaaɠe households may come into being and be nurtured through their period of inevitable non-viability through the agency of the household heads' fathers, this is not invariably the case, and a brother or father's brother's family may act as a quasi-paternal household. In these cases the conditions governing the non-viability of the newly formed household are the same. But there are significant differences in the control exercised by the quasi-parent over loans of cattle. This control applies solely to father and son; a brother's son or brother is able to solicit loans in his own right as soon as his homestead and herd is established. Thus a household formed under the aegis of a brother or father's brother is more readily independent when shortage of cattle is in question.

In considering the causes of non-viability of families it has been shown that this is adjusted in various ways. At the inception of a family its inevitable non-viability is met by co-residence and co-operation with a household head who stands in a parental or quasi-parental relation to the head of the newly formed domestic unit. Subsequently, non-viability due to shortages of cattle are met by appeal to agnatic kinsmen. Potential shortages of humans are met by the processes of divorce and remarriage. Actual shortages of humans in the family is a matter of herdboys or dairymaids. Temporary help of girls is obtained by a woman among the unmarried girls of her agnatic lineage group. That of herdboys is obtained by temporary co-residence of households whose heads are agnatic kin. All these arrangements are designed to correct non-viability at the earliest opportunity, so that the simple or compound family may develop and exploit its means of subsistence in conditions which permit its greatest possible independence. This independence of economic action is secured for both men and women, and hence for the families to which they belong, by the help they can receive from agnatic kinsfolk.

In Woɗaaβe society, family development, in the sense of cyclical changes in the size and composition of viable domestic groupings based upon the family, must be regarded primarily as simple or compound family development. To the field observer this is readily obvious since dwelling units of a uniform pattern are referable to a simple or compound family as a household. More striking still is the association of herds with such family homesteads. Homesteads are grouped together, but this grouping is by no means indicative that they form joint domestic units. Where joint domestic units are formed, they are joint only in the limited sense of combining for the surveillance of cattle. Combinations of this sort are transitory and depend upon factors outside the formal development of the family. Only at the inception of a family are its formal properties likely to promote its incorporation into a wider domestic unit, that of father and son, father's brother and brother's son, or of brothers. The duration and degree of dependence exhibited in these joint households varies with the state of development of the parental or quasi-parental family; indeed where the parental family is well endowed, the initial non-viability of a filial household may be completely nullified.

This fragmentation into domestic units based upon the simple or compound family is made possible primarily by an inheritance system which, in the main, throughout a man's life matches the means of subsistence to which he has title, or which he actively controls, to his own skill and strength as a herdsman or begetter of herdsmen.

This family system may be regarded as an adaptation to a set of particular natural conditions in which seasonal variations and irregular natural hazards, as well as the social environment, encourage a high degree of autonomy in the smallest social units.

NOTES

[1] Fieldwork in west Bornu was carried out in 1951–2 and again for a short period in 1953. Comparative studies were made in other widely separate areas—Pankshin Division in Plateau Province, and Maska District in Katsina Emirate. These studies in no way invalidate the conclusions reached here, but a detailed comparison of the different ranges of ecological, demographic and social factors involved must be reserved for a later publication. I carried out fieldwork in all three areas as a Travelling Scholar of the Worshipful Company of Goldsmiths, with the further assistance of a grant from the Colonial Social Science Research Council, administered by the Government of Nigeria. I gratefully acknowledge the generosity of these bodies, and the kindness of their representatives.

[2] In the context of the homestead, west is synonymous with 'front', and east with 'back'; these pairs of terms are used here interchangeably as in Fulani linguistic usage. 'Left' and 'right' are not used for north and south in this context, and I have kept to Fulani usage. North is on the left-hand of the observer as he stands facing the homestead.

[3] Cf. Ar. *Iddah*. The period of continence or mourning prescribed by Islamic Law. The *edda* of a widow is four months and ten days, and, if she is pregnant, longer than this period, until her delivery. The *edda* of a *divorcée* is three lunar months: if she is pregnant, until delivery, either before or after the expiry of the three-month period. (Vesey-Fitzgerald, *Muhammedan Law*, London, 1931: 52).

CONCERNING TROBRIAND CLANS AND THE KINSHIP CATEGORY 'TABU'

By E. R. LEACH

For social anthropologists Malinowski's ethnographic accounts of Trobriand Island culture are a kind of Domesday Book. Palpably incomplete, palpably imperfect, they yet transcend in some indefinable way everything of like kind. This paper is an attempt to demonstrate from Malinowski's own material that certain of his inferential conclusions were incorrect. It is with no feelings of disrespect that I offer this revision. On the contrary I consider it a tribute to Malinowski's remarkable skill as an ethnographer that he can be shown to have recorded important features of the Trobriand social system of which he himself was unaware. The conclusion which I reach at the end of my paper is a functional one which would have appealed strongly to Malinowski's imagination.

The paper has originated in this way. In an essay contributed to a forth-coming critical symposium on Malinowski's writings (Firth 1957) I have argued that Malinowski's emphasis on the pragmatic consequences of behaviour led him to underestimate the degree to which behaviour can serve as a system of symbolic communication. I have cited his view that classifica-tory kinship terminologies are to be explained as systems of homonyms as an example of the sociological distortion that results from this kind of prag-matism. The present paper elaborates this argument in detail.

Like the other contributions to this volume my paper bears a certain genetic relationship to Fortes's essay 'Time and Social Structure' (Fortes 1949(a)). The common theme is that the nature of a social system can only be fully understood when we recognize adequately that any particular individual occupies successively a series of different positions in the total structure.

In brief, the problems which I seek to answer are these. First, why do the Trobrianders have four clans?

The common sense explanation is that it is an historical accident. That no doubt is the explanation which Malinowski himself would have offered. That seems to me too simple.

As a matter of fact Malinowski fails to explain why the Trobrianders should have a clan system at all. The clans appear to play no social role as such. The effective social groupings in Trobriand society are the units which Malinowski calls sub-clans. It is these sub-clans which are the landowning units, and which operate efficiently as exogamous corporations. Yet, according to Malinowski, each of these numerous sub-clans is allocated to one or other of four totemic clans, and the number four is, it seems, important:

Humanity is divided into four clans. Totemic nature is conceived to be as deeply ingrained in the substance of the individual as sex, colour, and stature. It can never be changed, and it transcends individual life, for it can be carried over into the next world, and brought back into this one when the spirit returns by reincarnation. This fourfold totemic division is thought to be universal, embracing every section of mankind... (Malinowski 1932: 416).

To use Malinowski's terminology, this is quite clearly a 'mythical charter' for something or other. But for what? Malinowski does not explain; I shall seek to do so.

My second problem concerns the tantalizing Trobriand word *tabu* which Malinowski discusses at some length on several occasions (Malinowski 1932: 423, 450–1; 1935, II: 28, 113).

Malinowski distinguishes several meanings of this word which he regards as homonyms—i.e. as different words of similar sound. Apparently he considered that there were at least three such distinct words:

1. *tabu* = taboo, sacred, forbidden. This, according to Malinowski, is an alien word introduced into the Trobriands by Christian missionaries.

2. *tabu* = grandparents, ancestors, totems.

3. *tabu* = father's sister and, by a process of extension, 'lawful woman' —i.e. a woman with whom sexual intercourse is permitted.

On Malinowski's own showing *tabu* in the Trobriands also has various further meanings, e.g. grandchild, and 'husband of any lawful woman'. It is not clear to me whether Malinowski regarded these as yet further homonyms or as extended meanings of the first three.

Now homonyms occur in most languages and, since Malinowski was a most notable linguist, we should perhaps accept his views on the matter. But this I prefer not to do. I submit the hypothesis that Malinowski was here mistaken and that there is only one Trobriand word *tabu*, all the meanings of which are closely and logically connected.

Finally I shall show how my 'solutions' to these two 'problems' tie in very nicely with a third curiosity of Trobriand ethnography, the celebrated origin myth, whereby various original ancestors are made to emerge from holes in the ground conveniently situated at known sites on ancestral property. In pursuing these inquiries we shall be led to re-examine and partly reinterpret Malinowski's views concerning the nature of Trobriand rules of incest and exogamy.

Let us start by considering the various meanings of *tabu*, regarded as a kinship category. In Malinowski's published writings there is no complete list of Trobriand kinship terminology. The nearest approximation to such a list is to be found in *The Sexual Life of Savages*, ch. XIII, section 6. However, in preparing this paper I have had the advantage of being able to consult Mr H. A. Powell, who carried out anthropological fieldwork in the Trobriand Islands in 1950–1. Mr Powell has not only filled in the gaps in Malinowski's kinship term diagram, he has also explained how in certain particulars Malinowski's diagram is in error. The points at which I rely on Mr Powell's information in lieu of Malinowski's own are noted in the text below.

I must stress that I have used Mr Powell simply as an informant on matters of fact. My use of his material does not in any way imply that he agrees with my theoretical interpretations; indeed I know very well that he does not. For all that, his comments on a preliminary draft of this paper have been extremely helpful.

Considered simply as a system in itself, without regard to cultural context, Trobriand kinship terminology falls into the well-known Crow type which has long been recognized as correlated in a general way with matrilineal descent (Tax 1937: 12 ff.). There are, however, a number of atypical features —e.g. Ego's mother's brother's wife falls into the same term category as Ego's mother. As a consequence, the system as a whole cannot be made comprehensible by a simple lineage analysis of the kind favoured by Radcliffe-Brown and his pupils (e.g. Gilbert 1937: 292). Instead of arguing *a priori* let us then start with Malinowski's own analysis.

As I have already indicated, Malinowski's treatment of the term *tabu*, regarded as a kinship term, starts by distinguishing *tabu* meaning grandmother and *tabu* meaning father's sister as two different words. Of the latter he says:

The primary meaning of this word [*tabu*] is 'father's sister'. It also embraces 'father's sister's daughter' or 'paternal cross cousin' or by extension 'all the women of the father's clan'; and, in its widest sense 'all the women not of the same clan [as Ego]'. In this, its most extensive application, the word stands for 'lawful woman'..... For such a woman the term *lubaygu*, 'my sweetheart', may be correctly used; but this term is absolutely incompatible with the kinship designation, *lu(gu)ta*, 'my sister'. This linguistic use embodies, therefore, the rule of exogamy, and to a large extent expresses the ideas underlying this (Malinowski 1932: 423).

On Malinowski's own showing, this statement is neither comprehensive nor altogether accurate. It ignores the fact that the category *tabu*, regarded as a kinship term, is used by members of both sexes and that, in either case, it includes numerous males as well as females. It is true that most 'lawful' (i.e. 'marriageable') women are classed as *tabu* by a male Ego, but this does not equate, as Malinowski seems to suggest, with 'all women not of the same clan as Ego'. On the contrary, both the wives and the daughters of the men of both Ego's own sub-clan and that of his father are ordinarily categorized by terms other than *tabu*, and this is true also of a large number of other women who, in later life, are connected affinally to Ego through his wife.

Throughout his analysis Malinowski assumes that 'prohibitions on sexual intercourse' and 'rules of exogamy' are interchangeable, coincident, descriptions of the same set of regulations; moreover, in the context cited, he states explicitly that by 'exogamy' he means 'clan incest'. In Malinowski's presentation the exogamous group is defined by the principle of matrilineal descent alone and is influenced by no other factor. His argument is that, in its widest extension, the category *tabu* serves to mark off this exogamous grouping—the women who are *tabu* are the 'lawful women' who are outside the barrier of clan incest. Using exogamy in this sense Malinowski's explanation simply fails to fit the facts which he describes.

But what better explanation can be offered?

It is a cardinal and fundamental assumption in Malinowski's analysis that words employed in kinship terminology have attached to them certain *primary* meanings and sentiments, which derive from a sociological relationship existing between the speaker and a particular individual near-kinsman. The use of kinship terms in a classificatory sense comes about through the gradual extension of these primary sentiments to a wider and wider range of individuals. Thus, to take a particular instance, the term *tama*, which a Trobriander ultimately applies to nearly all the males of his father's clan, has, in Malinowski's view, the *primary* meaning 'father' or 'mother's husband' and all extended uses of the term are derived from the initial relationship existing between a Trobriand father and his son (Malinowski 1932: 5).

In my own analysis I shall make no such assumption. I do not repudiate the possibility of the 'extension' of meanings from narrow primary to wider secondary contexts, but I do not admit that words used as kinship terms must, *ipso facto*, derive their primary meaning exclusively from a kinship context, nor that the primary application is always to a particular individual rather than to a class of individuals.

For example, I agree with Malinowski that the term *tama* has a primary meaning which later undergoes extension, but, where Malinowski supposes that the primary meaning stems from the context of the nuclear family, so that *tama*='mother's husband', I myself would suggest that the primary meaning here stems from the identification of a particular group of males with a particular locality. My own 'primary' translation would be *tama*= 'domiciled male of my father's sub-clan hamlet'. Let me elaborate this distinction.

I fully accept Malinowski's contention that, of all the males whom the child addresses as *tama*, the speaker's own father is the one with whom Ego has the most personal contacts, but that does not make 'father' the primary meaning of *tama*, nor does it imply that every *tama* is looked upon as being, in some sense, 'a kind of father'. The fact that I have a pet dog called Peter, does not make Peter the primary meaning of the word *dog*, nor does it imply that I cannot distinguish between my dog and another.

My view is that most words employed in kinship terminologies are category terms rather than individualizing proper names. Malinowski insisted that *tama* refers primarily to a particular individual, the father, and to other individuals only by extension; he supposed that any other view would imply that Trobrianders cannot distinguish between one *tama* and another (Malinowski 1932: 447). My own assumption, on the contrary, is that *tama* refers primarily to a category; this does not imply any suggestion that Trobrianders have any difficulty about distinguishing the roles of different individual *tama*.

Malinowski does not describe for us in detail the actual kinship composition of any particular Trobriand local community, but he explains fairly clearly what the ideal 'theoretical' composition of such a community ought to be according to the Trobrianders' own ideas. Land in the Trobriands is owned by the matrilineal sub-clans (Malinowski 1932: 26, 417; 1935, 1: ch. XII). The married males of the sub-clan, numbering it would seem about a dozen individuals, live, each in his own domestic household, in a village, or section of a village, situated on or near the sub-clan land. I shall call this collectivity a sub-clan hamlet.

Here let me emphasize two things. First, the assertion that all the adult males of a sub-clan live in their own sub-clan hamlet is almost certainly an idealization of reality. I imagine that in almost all actual cases there are some married men who are *not* living in the hamlet of their own sub-clan. But this discrepancy between fact and ideal does not, I think, affect my argument. Secondly, my phrase 'sub-clan hamlet' is not meant to be identical with the term 'village' as used by Malinowski.

In Malinowski's writings 'village' ordinarily means the cluster of buildings around a particular central place (*baku*). Although such a 'village' may sometimes be occupied by householders of a single sub-clan, this is not ordinarily the case.

The more usual pattern is that a village comprises several sections each of which is associated with a different sub-clan. The households forming one section of the village belong to married males of one particular sub-clan, and these men collectively exercise certain rights of ownership over parts of the garden land adjacent to the village. The houses in a village section plus the garden lands associated with this village section form a unity which I call a sub-clan hamlet. This analysis is valid even though the houses and gardens of different sections of the same village are immediately adjacent to one another.

In these terms, the 'component village of Yalumugwa' (Malinowski 1935, 1: 385) embraces two sub-clan hamlets; Omarakana (1935, 1: 430) comprises three sub-clan hamlets, though in this case the male householders of one of the three sub-clans reside in another village. My phrase 'sub-clan hamlet' equates therefore with Malinowski's 'village section' and appears to correspond to a native Trobriand category (1935, 1: 430). The variety of land ownership rights that pertain to a sub-clan hamlet, considered as a corporation, is described in *Coral Gardens* (Malinowski 1935, 1: 343–4).

In the course of a lifetime both men and women are ordinarily resident members of two distinct sub-clan hamlets. A girl remains under the control of her parents until she marries, and then joins her husband in a new household established in the husband's sub-clan hamlet; at no stage is she a resident member of her own sub-clan hamlet. The pattern of residence for a boy is more complicated. He ceases to sleep in his parents' house at adolescence and joins a bachelor house (*bukumatulu*) (Malinowski 1932: 53–64). Bachelor houses are not necessarily identified as belonging to any particular sub-clan; boys of different sub-clans may sleep in one house. If a boy's father and his mother's brother live in different villages, he might, it seems, find bachelor accommodation in either community (Malinowski 1935, 1: 36, 205, 357). But a boy only sleeps in the bachelor house, he does not eat there.

From an early age a boy plays his part in garden work, but while he starts by working for his father he gradually transfers his productive effort to his mother's brother's lands (1935, 1: 60, 191). So long as he contributes directly to his parents' household, he receives food from his mother; when he contributes to his mother's brother's household, he receives food from his mother's brother's wife. The economic consequences of this shift are small, for when the boy works on his mother's brother's land, the produce serves to increase the annual harvest gift (*urigubu*) which the mother's brother's household contributes to the father's household. Thus, in either case, the boy may be said to be working for his parents.

Finally, on marriage, a young man establishes a new independent household in his own sub-clan hamlet. From his garden plots he continues to make *urigubu* payments to his parents and his married sisters.

I must emphasize that although a boy ceases to sleep in his parents' house at adolescence he does not fully renounce his residence rights there until after he is married. Marriage itself is publicly established by the act of cohabitation in the household of the boy's father—*not* that of his mother's brother (Malinowski 1932: 75, 93).

We may describe all this by saying that, in the precise terminology of English law, a Trobriand male is, from the start, *domiciled* in his own sub-clan hamlet but his *residence* varies. During childhood he is resident in his father's sub-clan hamlet; after marriage he is resident in his own sub-clan hamlet; during the interval between adolescence and marriage he has a dual status with residence rights in both communities.

These facts provide the core of my analysis. My thesis is that, as a child, the male Ego identifies himself primarily with his father's household while, as an adult, he identifies himself primarily with the members of his own sub-clan hamlet considered as a corporation. I argue that this time shift in the composition and membership of the group whom Ego (male) regards as 'people like us' is fundamental for our understanding of the nature of Trobriand kinship categories.

The position of a girl is different; though technically domiciled in her own sub-clan hamlet, she is never actually resident there. The analysis which follows is pursued solely from the viewpoint of a male Ego. A separate though comparable analysis would be necessary to explain the system of kinship categories used by a girl.

It follows from what I have said, and from Malinowski's own description of the sex and age categories in Trobriand society (Malinowski 1932: 51), that any particular sub-clan hamlet, at any particular time, comprises the following categories of individuals:

A Old men—*tomwaya* or *toboma*.[1]

B Old women—*numwaya*—wives of A, widows, etc.

C Active married men—*tovavaygile*.

D Active married women—*navavaygile*—wives of C.

E Bachelors—*to'ulatile*—'sister's sons' to A and C and resident here only part of the time.

F Young girls—*inagwadi*—and adolescent girls—*nakapugula*—still under the charge of their parents, daughters of A, B, C, D.

G Young boys—*gwadi*—still living with their parents—sons of A, B, C, D.

In this classification A, C and E together comprise the locally resident owners of the sub-clan hamlet. In addition, some other male members of the sub-clan, young boys, live scattered about among other hamlets with their parents. B, D, F and G in the above classification are all members of 'alien' sub-clans; that is to say, although their *residence* is in this hamlet, their *domicile* is elsewhere.

Let us now ignore altogether Malinowski's tendentious arguments about the way in which kinship sentiments are first established within the context of the elementary family and then extended outwards. Instead let us simply consider from first principles how a Trobriander might reasonably be expected to classify his kinsmen and acquaintance.

It seems evident from Malinowski's account that the two really fundamental economic facts in Trobriand social organization are (a) an individual's rights to the use or produce of the land of his or her own sub-clan, and (b) the institution of *urigubu* which results from this principle of land tenure. Rights in the land are possessed by men and women alike, but only the men of the sub-clan have direct access to their land. The men therefore cultivate the land; one major share (*taytumwala*) of the produce is kept by the cultivator for the use of his own household and for seed purposes; another, usually larger, share (*urigubu*) is transferred in harvest gifts to the cultivator's mother and married sisters (Malinowski 1935, 1: 194). Let us assume that these economic facts are the ones which provide the primary criteria for distinguishing categories of kin.

It is plain that the individual Trobriand male experiences the effects of the *urigubu* institution in two distinct phases; first, as a child in his father's household, and secondly, as a married adult in his own household.

In the first phase the implications of *urigubu*-giving are lopsided. The child is a member of a household which regularly receives gifts from members of a sub-clan hamlet which he is taught from the start to regard as his own. These people, his 'mother's brothers' (*kada*), are clearly, in a formal sense, 'friends'. The friendship may indeed be subject to strain, but it is palpably advantageous to 'our household'.

In contrast, a substantial share of the produce of his own father's garden is given away to strangers—the father's mother and the father's sister—from whom Ego receives no benefits. On the contrary, in the long run, the sons of these strangers will appear on the scene and usurp the property which at present seems to be the main source of Ego's livelihood. These people too no doubt are, officially speaking, to be regarded as 'friends', but from Ego's point of view they are very disadvantageous ones. Indeed in many respects these strangers, the recipients of the father's *urigubu* gifts, might seem to be the prototype 'enemy'.

I shall here digress to remind the reader briefly of certain features of Radcliffe-Brown's theoretical discussions of taboo and joking relationships (Radcliffe-Brown 1952: chs. IV, V, VII).

For Radcliffe-Brown *taboo* is a technical term with a narrower range of meaning than the common Polynesian word *tabu*. He discusses taboo in terms of what he calls 'ritual avoidances' which serve to define the 'ritual status' differences existing between two persons in a single social system. The following are some of the characteristics of taboo which emerge from Radcliffe-Brown's analysis: Tabooed persons are respected as sacred, they are the object of ritual avoidance and the recipients of tribute. The tabooed thing or person is 'abnormal', it is separated from that which is normal, but its quality is ambivalent; it is a source of power, but the power may have good or evil consequences, it is sacred and polluting at the same time.

The ritual behaviours which Radcliffe-Brown discusses under the general title of 'joking relationships' are an exemplification of this theme. These behaviours express 'friendship' either by manifesting taboo—e.g. ritual avoidance coupled with gift-giving—or else by the systematic breach of taboo, which amounts to much the same thing—for, in Radcliffe-Brown's argument, anyone who breaks a taboo automatically becomes taboo himself. That taboo should be used in this way to express 'friendship' is the subject of one of Radcliffe-Brown's most penetrating pieces of analysis.

He points out that marriage often serves to unite two potentially hostile groups, and that it then becomes necessary for members of these 'opposed' parties to assert, by formal behaviour, that they are 'friends'. The 'friendship' involved is of a peculiar and precariously balanced kind: it is 'a relation neither of solidarity nor of hostility but of "friendship" in which the separateness of the groups is emphasized, but open conflict between the two groups or members on the two sides is avoided'. By way of example he refers to his own description of the Andamanese *aka-yat* relationship (Radcliffe-Brown 1933: 81) in which two individuals who scrupulously avoid one another constantly send each other presents. There seems an obvious parallel here with the Trobriand householder who avoids his married sister yet regularly sends her gifts.

Radcliffe-Brown further points out that the kind of ritual friendship which may characterize the behaviour of persons linked by ties of affinity is also frequently characteristic of the behaviour that is expected between members of alternating generations—e.g. between a grandparent and a grandchild —the fact that in some societies a man is expected to marry his 'classificatory granddaughter' exemplifies this similarity (Radcliffe-Brown 1952: 79–80, 100).

Radcliffe-Brown's discussion is here not altogether convincing. Since he treats the relationship between grandparents and grandchildren as an example of joking relationship, one might infer that the friendship involved is one in which 'there is an appearance of antagonism, controlled by conventional rules' (1952: 112), yet elsewhere he has maintained that 'in many classificatory systems the terms for grandfather and grandmother are used...as implying a general attitude of friendliness, relatively free from restraint towards all persons to whom they are applied' (1952: 79).

This contradiction disappears if we say that 'friendliness' and 'hostility' are not, properly speaking, exclusive categories; as with the case of 'sacred-ness' and 'pollution', each is an aspect of 'the same thing'. Radcliffe-Brown's argument would have been more convincing if he had simply opposed 'relations of solidarity', which stem from economic co-operation and common economic interest, and 'relations of separateness', which link persons who are outside this co-operative corporation. His essential theme is that all relations of this latter kind have an ambivalent friendship/hostility content; they are always formally expressed by behaviours indicating 'friendship' but, in especially critical situations, an added element of taboo is present, super-imposed on the friendliness. From this digression let us now return to the Trobriand Islands.

That the relationship which links groups of Trobriand affines in bonds of 'friendship' is of a precarious kind is plain enough. Malinowski himself describes the relationship between a man and his father's sister's son as one of 'predestined enmity' (Malinowski 1932: 13). This latent hostility becomes explicitly formalized in the mortuary rituals which follow the death of either the father's sister or her husband or that of either of the father's parents. On these occasions not only are the affinally linked sub-clans ritually opposed to one another in the clearest possible manner, but the affines of the deceased are very liable to be accused of murder by sorcery. 'It is characteristic of their idea of the bonds of marriage and fatherhood—which they regard as artificial and untrustworthy under any strain—that the principle suspicion of sorcery attaches always to the wife and children' (1932: 137).

The male Ego's own role in this situation is by no means clear cut. As a member of his mother's sub-clan, he is an affine of his father, and thus a kind of logical ally of his father's other affines, who come near to being his father's enemies. My thesis is, however, that the young child, resident in his father's house, is taught to accept a set of kinship categories which are appropriate to the structural situation of that household. In that situation the recipients of Ego's father's *urigubu* form a highly ambivalent category of kinsmen.

Enemies who must be treated as 'friends'; dangerous people who must be appeased by gift giving; this precisely is the context which, in Radcliffe-Brown's terminology, reflects a situation of taboo.

In Radcliffe-Brown's terms, the relationship which Malinowski describes as existing between the givers and receivers of *urigubu* is one of taboo. Consistent with this we find that a man's child is taught to class as *tabu* all the recipients of his father's *urigubu*. The category *tabu* includes:

(*a*) Ego's father's mother.
(*b*) Her husband and the other males of his sub-clan.
(*c*) Ego's father's sister.
(*d*) Her husband and the other males of her sub-clan.
(*e*) The daughters of (*a*) and (*d*).

Accordingly, instead of postulating, as Malinowski does, that the Trobrianders have several different words pronounced *tabu* I assume that they have only one such word and that its meaning approximates to Radcliffe-Brown's concept of taboo.

Malinowski tells us little of the prescribed behaviour that accompanies this verbal category, though it appears that, as Ego begins to grow up, he finds himself in an emphatic joking relationship with his father's sister (Malinowski 1932: 450). On my thesis, it is not to be expected that a male Ego will be required to behave in exactly the same way towards all his *tabu*. In Radcliffe-Brown's terminology 'joking relationship' or 'ritual friendship' includes not only violent and obscene horseplay between cross-cousins but also playful friendliness between grandparents and grandchildren. If then the Trobriand relationship *tabu* is likewise one of 'ritual friendship', there is room for variation.

What seems to happen is that while Ego (male) is still a child in his father's household his 'friendship' with the immediate recipients of his father's *urigubu* is critical enough to involve a relationship of the 'obscene joking'

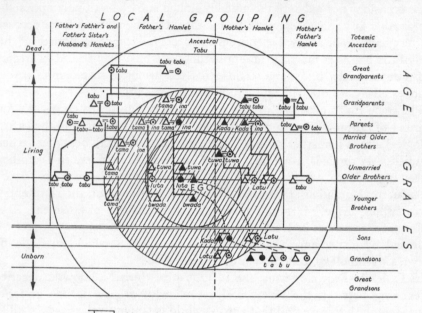

Fig. 1

Innermost circle—classificatory siblings—*tuwa, bwada, luta.*
Middle ring—*tama, ina, kada, latu.*
Outermost ring—*tabu.*
All within the shaded circle are 'socially close' to Ego either
  on account of common domicile or common residence.
All *tabu* are 'socially distant' from Ego either on account of
  difference in age or difference in residence.

type. But as he grows older and begins to separate off from his father's household, the social distance between himself and these paternal *tabu* steadily increases. Such *tabu* are still 'formal friends' but the stereotype of behaviour now becomes one of playful friendliness rather than obscene horseplay. On this basis the father's sister's daughter is said to be an appropriate object for sexual liaison and ultimate marriage (1932: 295). I shall have more to say concerning this alleged 'preferred marriage' presently.

The young male Ego's *tabu* category is not confined to the recipients of his father's *urigubu*. It extends also to a number of relatives distinguished by their age seniority and their social remoteness from Ego. Thus *tabu* includes Ego's mother's parents. In contexts which are not rigidly formal it also includes classificatory father's mother's mother's brothers and their wives, and classificatory mother's mother's brothers and their wives.[2] Note that it is social distance rather than genealogical distance that matters here. While Ego is resident with his father, it is only the males of the father's sub-clan who are *three* generations senior to Ego who may rate as *tabu*; that is to say individuals who are already, socially speaking, 'almost dead'. In contrast, the males of Ego's own sub-clan who are only *two* generations senior to himself may rate as *tabu*; but of course by the time Ego himself becomes a house-holder in his own sub-clan hamlet these too will be very old men withdrawn from social life. In relation to Ego all these elderly *tabu* are merging into the other-world of the sacred and ancestral dead.

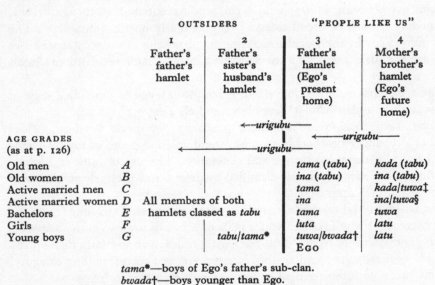

tama*—boys of Ego's father's sub-clan.
bwada†—boys younger than Ego.
tuwa‡—young married men of Ego's generation.
tuwa§—wives of men classed as tuwa (Source Powell).

Fig. 2

We can represent the whole system, as so far described, by a diagram (Fig. 1). Ego at the centre is surrounded by a body of 'near kinsmen', his father's group (*tama*) and his own sub-clan group (*kada*). Beyond this 'circle of active kin relations' in all directions lie the *tabu*, the marginal kin who merge into the outer unknown of dangerous strangers and dangerous ancestral spirits.

The same argument is presented in Fig. 2, which demonstrates even more clearly that the kinship categories express differences of locality and of age status rather than genealogical relationship.

In this figure the terms listed against the leading letters *A–G* correspond to the age categories listed above on p. 126. Ego (male), resident in his father's hamlet, is thought of as occupying a position at the bottom of col. 3. He classes all the members of his father's father's and father's sister's husband's hamlets as *tabu* except for a few young boys who are members of his own father's sub-clan. [3] He categorizes the members of his father's hamlet as in col. 3 and of his mother's hamlet as in col. 4 regardless of their sub-clan affiliation.

Although all the information contained in these diagrams is derived directly from the genealogically arranged table of kinship terms given by Malinowski himself (Malinowski 1932: 435), they suggest that the words involved have quite different 'primary meanings' from those given by Malinowski.

Tabu now appears as a general term, undifferentiated as to age or sex, comprising the whole broad category of potentially hostile 'outsiders'. The only individuals in the *urigubu*-receiving hamlets who are not categorized as *tabu* are the male *tama* who are domiciled in (and later residents of) Ego's father's hamlet.

Tama, as I have already suggested, is seen to refer to 'a domiciled male of my father's sub-clan hamlet' (see above and cf. Fortes 1953: 20).

Kada, tuwa, bwada are not here primarily 'mother's brother', 'elder brother', 'younger brother' but rather 'the domiciled males of my own sub-clan hamlet' categorized by age and generation. The use of *tuwa* and *bwada* for the wives of men previously classified by these terms is clearly an extension of the initial meaning.

Ina, which in Malinowski's analysis has the fundamental meaning 'mother', here becomes 'the wife of any senior male of either of my two home hamlets'.

Luta is not simply 'sister' but 'alien girls resident in my father's hamlet'. The phonemically very similar word *latu* represents a corresponding category, namely 'alien children resident in my own sub-clan hamlet'.

These last two terms need further discussion for they affect our understanding of incest and exogamy rules. For Malinowski the primary meaning of *luta* is 'own sister'; it is the fundamental incest category, 'the core of the *suvasova* taboo' (Malinowski 1932: 448). By 'extension' *luta* also comes to cover, first, a number of 'sub-clan sisters' who are regarded as real kinsmen (*veyola*) and to whom the *suvasova* taboo rigidly applies, and secondly, a much wider range of 'clan sisters' who are regarded as pseudo-kinsmen (*kakaveyola*) and to whom the *suvasova* taboo applies only in modified degree.

According to Malinowski, *marriage* with *luta* of all types is strictly prohibited but *sexual intercourse* with *luta* in the *kakaveyola* category, though 'prohibited by legal doctrine', 'is frequently practised, and is, so to speak, at a premium' (1932: 449). Unfortunately Malinowski entirely ignores the fact that most of the *luta* who are Ego's immediate next-door neighbours are not members of Ego's own sub-clan at all. This is true for example of the daughters of Ego's father born of wives other than Ego's own mother; and it is true also of most of the daughters of other males of Ego's father's sub-clan, all of whom are ordinarily resident close to Ego's own father. This is a very serious omission.

Malinowski makes a point of opposing the two categories *tabu* = 'lawful woman' and *luta* = 'prohibited woman' (1932: 423) but he couples this with a suggestion that *luta* are all 'clan sisters' and that it is the clan to which rules of exogamy and incest alike apply. But here he was surely either mistaken or misleading? The 'distant' *luta* with whom Ego is likely to be in most immediate contact, the girls with whom sex relations, though forbidden, are 'so to speak at a premium', are not his clan sisters scattered all over the island but the girls next door!

From Malinowski's elaborately detailed accounts of the amorous adventures of Trobriand childhood it appears that the sexual experiments of infancy and early adolescence are with local playmates. They are affairs which lack all seriousness. Now the most obvious playmates for a boy are the girls of his two home hamlets, the daughters of his *tama* and the daughters of his *kada*. It is surely striking that Ego rates the first as *luta*—'classificatory sisters' and the second as *latu*—'classificatory daughters'.

All members of the first of these categories fall, theoretically, under the incest prohibition (*suvasova*). Relations with the second category are not incestuous (*suvasova*) but they are nevertheless improper. According to Malinowski, marriage with such a girl 'is viewed with disfavour and happens only rarely'. The verbal similarity between the two terms perhaps reflects this similarity of valuations. Malinowski's statements, taken as a whole, imply that while a boy can safely have love affairs with any of his *latu* and most of his neighbouring *luta*, he can decently marry neither.

In contrast, serious love affairs of the kind likely to lead to marriage tend to be with girls of other hamlets, most of whom fall into the *tabu* category (Malinowski 1932: 295). Affairs of this latter type are described in section 6 of ch. IX of *The Sexual Life of Savages*. In some cases they evidently entail a substantial element of risk for the lovers and were formerly the occasion of para-military raiding parties, especially if the girls concerned lived outside the local village cluster.

In all, we are left with two equations:

(a) The girls of Ego's two home hamlets—classed like 'sisters' and 'daughters'—mostly fair game for a love affair, but not suitable for marriage —*luta* and *latu*.

(b) The girls outside Ego's two home hamlets—classed like 'potential enemies'—suitable for marriage—*tabu*.

This is a conclusion which would have satisfied Tylor (White 1948: 416; Tylor 1888: 267). It suggests quite a different picture from that given by Malinowski. In his interpretation, all pre-marital sex relations are to be regarded as trial preliminaries leading to marriage. For Malinowski the typical youthful love affair is with a *tabu*, the 'lawful woman'. Yet I feel he must be wrong. The structure that I have now presented has so many striking parallels in other societies (e.g. Fortes 1949(*b*): 249; Evans-Pritchard 1951: 44–8), and it makes sense in so many different ways.

Malinowski's analysis rests on the assumption that the fundamental element in the total system is 'clan exogamy'; but Trobriand clans are shadowy amorphous things with no very obvious function. Why and how should such shadowy entities maintain their exogamy? In contrast, the membership of sub-clan hamlets is clear and corporate and economically highly significant. I find it very illuminating to realize that if a Trobriander keeps to the rules which Malinowski describes it is not merely Ego's clan that becomes exogamous; it is the total population of Ego's two home hamlets that is set apart as 'people like us' (see Fig. 2, p. 131).

Let me emphasize again that these 'hamlets' are not spacially separate entities immediately discernible on the ground. A single village may contain households of a number of different sub-clans and the members of these sub-clans inter-marry. But the hamlets are defined as entities by the rules of exogamy and the category distinctions of kinship terminology. I have already quoted Malinowski as saying 'this linguistic usage (with respect to *luta*) embodies therefore the rule of exogamy and to a large extent expresses the ideas underlying this' (see p. 122). I would now agree with this but it is the exogamy of local grouping that I am talking about whereas Malinowski thought only of the exogamy of clans.

As to how far the *luta* category—as I have now distinguished it—forms, in fact, an exogamous category, I have no information. That it is ideally considered to be such seems clearly apparent in Malinowski.

The distinction I have now made between casual premarital love affairs with *luta* and *latu*, and serious liaisons with *tabu*, is fully consistent with the kind of meaning I have already attributed to the word *tabu*. It eliminates a striking inconsistency in Malinowski's presentation which makes it appear that marriage, a contractual arrangement of the most serious economic consequences, is the legal outcome of love affairs of the utmost casualness.

In terms of my diagram *latu* are 'the children of the married males of Ego's own sub-clan'. A category of this type is to be expected in any 'Crow-type' system of kinship terminology. Malinowski translates it simply as 'child' (Malinowski 1932: 434–6).

As the Trobriand male child grows up he begins to separate himself off from his parents and for a while has a kind of dual residential status in both his home hamlets—that of his father and that of his mother's brother. During this phase there is little change in the way that Ego's kinsmen are categorized, but the significance of the different categories becomes modified. For example, in terms of Radcliffe-Brown's analysis which I outlined above, the relationship between Ego and his father which was formerly one of 'solidarity' now begins to assume the qualities of 'separateness' and ritual 'friendship', while, on the other hand, the relationship of Ego with the senior males of his own sub-clan, which had previously been one of 'friendship' and 'separateness' now changes to one of 'solidarity'.

It is symptomatic of this change of attitude that Ego who has previously referred to the householders of his own sub-clan hamlet collectively as *kada* (uncles) now begins to refer to the same collectivity as *tuwa* (brothers) (Mr Powell's information).

At the same time Ego's father's affines (Ego's paternal *tabu*) move outside the field of Ego's *urigubu* system altogether, they now become remote relatives barely distinguishable from total strangers (*tomakava*). Meanwhile many of the elders of his own sub-clan hamlet will have died. These men, whom Ego referred to as *tabu* while he was living with his father, remain *tabu* even though they now exist only in the world of ancestral spirits.

When finally the Trobriand male Ego marries and settles down the *urigubu* institution assumes for him a new significance. Ego is now resident in his own sub-clan hamlet along with his mother's brother. He is receiving gifts from his wife's brother's hamlet and he is also linked in ties of friendly alliance with his wife's father's hamlet—which was his wife's original home. In turn he is giving gifts to his sister's husband and to his father in the latter's capacity as mother's husband.

At this phase in the boy's development the *urigubu* can no longer be considered as an isolated institution; it is closely enmeshed with the political relationships which bind a man to his chief; it is linked through the institutionalized payments called *youlo* and *takola* with the prestige-gaining activities of the *kula* exchange; it is part of 'a veritable tangle of obligations and duties' which are finally worked out only after the death of the *urigubu* recipients (Malinowski, 1935, 1: 56, 406, 190, 372; 1932, 136; 1922: 64). It is Malinowski's thesis that the *urigubu* gifts which a man makes to the husbands of his mother and his sisters are adequately reciprocated by the various benefits, political and otherwise, which he receives in return. Malinowski does not make it very clear just why a Trobriander should have this evaluation, but we must accept the fact that it is so.

It is a symptom of this equality between givers and receivers of *urigubu* that at every phase Ego is, terminologically, in a reciprocal relationship with all the members of his *urigubu* system, other than his own father. As a child Ego classes the recipients of his father's *urigubu* as *tabu* and the givers of his father's *urigubu* as *kada*, both terms are used reciprocally. Now as an adult he uses the term *lubou* both for his sister's husband to whom he himself gives *urigubu* and for his wife's brother from whom he receives *urigubu*. The other males of the sister's husband's sub-clan who are also indirect beneficiaries of Ego's *urigubu* payments fall into the *yawa* category, which is again a reciprocal term.

Marriage establishes a *lubou* relationship between two men, namely the wife's brother and her husband. This relationship is expressed by the payment of *urigubu*. The same marriage puts the hamlets with which the two *lubou* are associated in a vaguer affinal relationship signified by the reciprocal use of the kinship category *yawa*.

The marriage of a male Ego and the marriage of his sister thus puts Ego in affinal relationship with the members of four hamlets—those of his wife's mother's brother, his wife's father, his sister's husband, and more vaguely his sister's husband's father. Nearly all these relatives are *yawa*. [4] The only exceptions are *lubou's* brothers who are also *lubou*; *lubou's* children who are *tabu*, unless they are members of Ego's own clan when they are *kada*; and Ego's wife's unmarried sisters, who are classed as if they were male siblings (*tuwa/bwada*). Marriage with these last is not incestuous (*suvasova*) but is strongly disapproved (Malinowski 1932: 449), presumably because such polygyny would place a double load of *urigubu* liability on the one set of wives' brothers. Marriage with *kada* females is, of course, incestuous. Marriage with either *tabu* or *yawa* females is legitimate, though marriage with *tabu* is considered preferable.

Roughly speaking therefore the effect of marriage and its associated *urigubu* system is to create for Ego a new 'ring' of relatives which, in social distance, lie somewhere between the near kinsmen of the home groups and the distant marginal kinsmen classed as *tabu*. My Fig. 3 shows this argument schematically.

As in Fig. 1 Ego's total kinship system may still be thought of as a series of concentric circles centred about himself. But Ego is now located in the *kada/tuwa/bwada* group, while the *tama* are of declining significance. Indeed, by the time that both Ego's parents are dead the *tama* sub-clan will cease to be regarded as relatives at all.

Beyond the circle of these 'near kin', among whom Ego has residential status, are the affines (*lubou, yawa*), established as such by Ego's own marriage and the marriage of his sisters, and beyond them again are the marginal, socially remote, *tabu* relatives who lie outside Ego's personal system of *urigubu* transactions.

All the affines (*yawa* and *lubou*) are potentially hostile 'aliens' whose relationship is modified into a kind of treaty friendship by the fact of marriage and *urigubu* gift giving. It needs to be remembered that there is an avoidance relationship between a man and his sister, and though Malinowski is not very specific on the matter, it seems evident that the *lubou* relationship must be one of marked strain. So far as Ego is concerned, the relationship is based solely on the marriage bond and, if the marriage is terminated by death or divorce, the relationship is terminated also. Thereafter if the members of these affinal groups are categorized at all, they are rated simply as *tabu* or as 'total strangers' (*tomakava*) (Malinowski 1932: 4, 451; 1935, 1: 192).

At this stage in the male Ego's development the members of his father's hamlet are also drifting away into a relationship of weak affinity, though here

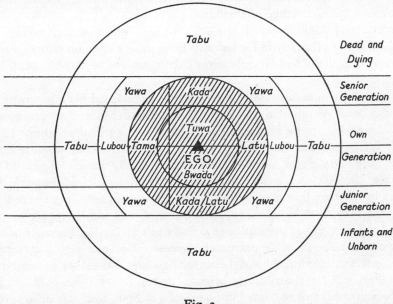

Fig. 3

the relationship link is less fragile than in the case of *lubou*. Even after their mother's death, sons will continue to make *urigubu* payments to their father. On the latter's death the sons have important duties to perform in the mortuary ritual (Malinowski 1935, 1: 192, 206). So long as either parent survives, a son cannot completely break off 'treaty relations' with his father's hamlet.

I must now make a somewhat lengthy digression to discuss Trobriand rules of preferred marriage. This is necessary not only because it has a bearing on the meaning of the term *tabu* but because it has been the subject of a good deal of unjustified theoretical speculation—as, for example, in Homans and Schneider (1955).

According to Malinowski, Trobrianders maintain a theoretical preference for marriage with the true father's sister's daughter. It is largely on the basis of this alleged preference that Malinowski bases his argument that *tabu* has the extended meaning 'lawful woman', for, in his view, this term refers primarily to the father's sister and her daughter who are, he says, 'the prototype' of the lawful woman (1932: 450).

The argument is unsatisfactory. Actual occurrences of patrilateral cross-cousin marriage seem to be rare and to be largely confined to the families of chiefs. Malinowski's only explanation of the rule is that it is a device whereby, in a matrilineal structure, a man, particularly a chief, may ultimately transmit his hereditary rights to his own son's son. He has not, however, demonstrated that Trobrianders themselves think of father's sister's daughter marriage as a tortuous legal subterfuge of this kind.

Nevertheless Malinowski cites his Trobriand informants as saying: 'the true *tabu* is the proper wife for us' and he is most emphatic that this means marriage with the *actual* father's sister's daughter (1932: 81, 86, 451). What are we to make of this?

It is of course possible that Malinowski misunderstood his informants, and that they were merely maintaining that most actual marriages are between individuals who are in a *tabu* relationship of one kind or another. This of course is true enough. The rules of exogamy exclude women who are classed as *ina*, *luta*, *latu*, *tuwa*, *bwada*, *kada* and this only leaves *yawa* and *tabu* available. But let us consider what would be implied if Malinowski were correct in thinking that marriage with the first cousin *tabu* is preferred.

On the face of it, a marriage convention of this kind appears to be in direct conflict with the principles of *urigubu* gift giving. If normal residence behaviour is adhered to, a patrilateral cross-cousin marriage will serve to cancel out the economic bond between Ego and his father's community. While Ego will be contributing *urigubu* to his father (*tama*), his father's sister's son (*tama*) will be contributing *urigubu* to Ego. Such direct reciprocity would make nonsense of the theme that *urigubu* payments represent, among other things, tribute from a political inferior to a political superior.

Moreover it is plain that direct reciprocity of this kind makes no sense to a Trobriander. When marriage with the true father's sister's daughter *does* occur, the residence pattern is abnormal. The husband, instead of taking his wife to live with him in his own sub-clan hamlet, acquires the right to settle in his wife's sub-clan hamlet and to farm his wife's land. In other words, he goes on living in his own father's village, and farms his father's land in company with his father's sister's sons (Malinowski 1932: 83, 86; 1935, 1: 206, 354, 385). According to Malinowski this comes about through the personal affection of a father for his son.

It is quite evident that such behaviour is altogether exceptional. The only example that Malinowski cites is that of a chief's son. Further, he states that if an ordinary commoner were to encroach in this way upon his *tama's* territorial privileges he would 'both degrade himself and suffer disabilities' (1932: 83 n.), which perhaps means that he would receive no *urigubu* from his wife's brothers.

Malinowski (1932: 85) does give a genealogy which is said to display three patrilateral cross-cousin marriages within one short pedigree, but in point of fact only one of these is between first cousins. Moreover, although Malinowski omits to mention the fact, the same genealogy also displays two (classificatory) *matrilateral* cross-cousin marriages; the chart therefore gives little support to the view that marriage with the true father's sister's daughter is preferred.

The genealogy in question is indeed revealing, but for reasons other than those suggested by Malinowski. Since the Tabalu chiefs receive their 'tribute' in the form of *urigubu* payments from their wives' brothers, it is a matter of some political significance as to who receives the *urigubu* payments of the chief himself. About this Malinowski tells us very little, but the cross-cousin marriages in his chart all have the effect of making members of the Kwoynama sub-clan recipients of the chief's *urigubu*. Elsewhere we are told that 'this sub-clan is the very one from which a Tabalu chief ought to choose his principal wife' (1932: 113–14). In doing so, he evidently marries a classificatory mother's brother's daughter (*latu*)—a relationship which is nearly incestuous (1932: 87). The implication seems to be that, as an exception to the normal system, a practice of *bilateral* cross-cousin marriage operates between the Kwoynama and Tabalu aristocratic sub-clans which permits these two groups to exchange *urigubu* gifts without prejudice to the political status of either.[5]

The principle involved can be stated thus. Whoever marries the sister of the chief's heir is potentially in a structurally superior position, for the chief's heir must give him tribute. By marrying this girl to his own son and then insisting that the son stays where he is, the chief is not 'favouring his son', he is protecting the rights of his heir! The son pays *urigubu* to his father the chief.

The reverse case is mentioned in a rather vague way by Malinowski (1935, 1: 362 f.). If a woman of high rank marries a man of lower rank, she may arrange for her son to marry the sister of her husband's heir. Again the son in question 'stays put' in his father's hamlet, instead of moving to his own. But in this case, unlike the first, he is able to transmit his irregularly acquired land rights to his own heirs—his sister's sons. This, according to Malinowski, is the mechanism whereby aristocratic sub-clans have been able to assert territorial claims in villages where they have no mythological roots.

On this analysis the preferred marriage with a father's sister's daughter, in so far as it exists, has nothing to do with the affection of fathers for their sons. It is simply a straightforward mechanism in the working of the political structure.

It is thus evident that, despite Malinowski, marriage with the 'true' *tabu* is exceptional. For anyone except the highest chiefs it is 'proper' (i.e. desirable) only in the sense that, if achieved, it permits the husband's sub-clan to encroach on the land rights of the wife. It is a status-climbing device. On the other hand the fact that Trobriand chiefs contract marriage alliances which would be more or less taboo for everyone else is strictly in accord with theoretical expectations. (Radcliffe-Brown 1952: 138).

The system of terminology discussed above covers all the usage of a male Ego, for, as Ego grows older and acquires married children and grandchildren, the new relationships that are thereby set up are merely the reciprocals of those which Ego himself experienced as a youth. By the time that Ego and his sisters have married the various categories of relationship have received their final form.

Presented in this way the logic of the system is seen to be entirely simple and consistent. In contrast, when the terms are projected on to a genealogical diagram, as is done by Malinowski, the underlying logic is utterly incomprehensible. Anyone who doubts this opinion should compare the analysis given here with that given by Malinowski in *The Sexual Life of Savages*.

But while the term system is complete the diagrams cover the population of only eight particular sub-clan hamlets, namely:

(*a*) father's hamlet—male owners: *tama*,

(*b*) own hamlet—male owners: *kada, tuwa, bwada*,

(*c*) father's sister's husband's hamlet—male owners: *tabu*,

(*d*) father's father's hamlet—male owners: *tabu*,

(*e*) wife's brother's hamlet—male owners: *yawa, lubou*,

(*f*) wife's father's hamlet—male owners: *yawa*,

(*g*) sister's husband's hamlet—male owners: *yawa, lubou*,

(*h*) sister's husband's father's hamlet—male owners: *yawa*.

I suggest that this is in fact the initial range of effective kinship; it is the range of active *urigubu* transactions as they affect the individual Ego.

Just how far the various categories are 'extended' beyond this immediate operational context is not clear in Malinowski's writings. Evidently, in principle, all the terms applied to Ego's own sub-clan hamlet are applicable also to all other sub-clan hamlets of Ego's clan. Similarly the terms applied to the father's hamlet should apply also to all other hamlets of the father's clan and also to the hamlet of the mother's sister's husband and so on. But I suspect that much of this wider range of kinship is notional only. Where the category is in doubt the relationship is *tabu*.

Thus construed, the term *tabu*, as used by a male adult, becomes a category of purely marginal relationship. In Radcliffe-Brown's phrase (1952: 69)—'it is used to mark off a marginal region between non-relatives and those close relatives towards whom specific duties and over whom specific rights are recognised'. It is a negative category (Malinowski 1935, II: 113). *Tabu* comprises all those numerous members of Ego's total society who are *not* in one way or another directly involved in the *urigubu* transactions of which Ego is either giver or receiver.

In terms of genealogy some *tabu* appear to be quite 'closely related'— e.g. the father's sister, the father's parents, the mother's parents. But in terms of structure these people are scarcely relatives at all. The households of which they are members are, socially speaking, remote from Ego; he has virtually no economic contact with them. Only the father's sister, with whom there is a formal joking relationship, is close enough to be regarded as in some respects a member of 'our group'.

Remote kinship is not only vague but ambiguous. According to Mr Powell: 'Kinship terms are used only in contexts where emphasis is on the formal aspects of kinship relations; in ordinary conversation personal names are used more frequently between, and of, persons of all ages and both sexes.' The occasions on which one would require to specify the precise kinship category of a distant clan relative must be rare. The uncertainty as to whether a distant clansman should be regarded as a clan relative (*kada, tuwa, bwada*), some sort of affine (*tama, yawa, lubou*), or scarcely a relative at all (*tabu*), is thus of no great consequence.

But this raises another issue which I mentioned at the beginning of this paper. Why do Trobrianders have a clan system at all? If, as seems to be the case, the operationally functional social groups are the sub-clans, what purpose do the clans serve, and why are there four of them?

In quite a different ethnographic context, that of the North Burma Kachins, I have pointed out that the assertion commonly made by Kachins that 'we have five clans' does not correspond to the empirical facts (Leach 1945). Nevertheless this assertion is a highly important schematic device. The Kachins need five distinct patrilineal categories if they are to explain to themselves the workings of their own society, and the fiction that there are only five clans altogether serves just this purpose. I suggest that in a comparable manner the Trobrianders need four categories to display the workings of their society, and that the four matriclans fulfil this purpose.

What happens in the Kachin case is that a Kachin will say *either* that the social world consists of five clans—Marip, Lahtaw, Lahpai, N'hkum, Maran *or* he will say that it consists of five major categories of kin: (i) *kahpu-kanau* (clan brothers), (ii) *mayu* (matrilateral affines), (iii) *dama* (patrilateral affines), (iv) *lawu* (classificatory grandchildren, 'those below'), (v) *lahta* (classificatory grandparents, 'those above'). Allowing for the fact that the Trobriands are matrilineal while the Kachins are patrilineal the corresponding categories in the Trobriand case would be (i) *kada, tuwa, bwada*, (ii) *tama*, (iii) *yawa/lubou*, (iv and v) *tabu*. Let me elaborate this.

On the analysis I have given in this paper it would appear that the individual Trobriand male is presented with a society which appears to consist of four distinct types of sub-clan hamlet. These are

A. People like us
- (a) *tama* hamlets
- (b) *kada, tuwa, bwada* hamlets

B. The others
- (c) affines: *yawa, lubou* hamlets
- (d) marginal relatives and non-relatives: *tabu* hamlets

From the individual Ego's point of view, this has the appearance of a moiety system. Ego should not seek a wife in (a) or (b); he should seek a wife in (c) or (d), especially perhaps in (d), since a marriage here will increase 'our' total range of kinship alliances. *Tabu* becomes the stereotype of a suitable wife simply because it is desirable in principle to reduce the number of *tabu* groups and convert them into *yawa*. Also, as I have indicated, a man who marries a *close tabu* may achieve a step up in the rank hierarchy.

Now these four categories of the total society are *not* unilineal descent groups. They are categories of hamlets distinguished according to the kind of people who are resident therein. Nevertheless I suggest that there is a functional connection between this fourfold categorization of Ego's kinship world and the fact that Trobrianders claim to have four clans.

The Trobriand myths of origin which form the basis of Trobriand rules of land tenure (Malinowski 1935, 1: 342 f.) specify that the original sub-clan ancestors emerged from various holes in the ground appropriately situated in the midst of sub-clan territory. It is these myths which establish that the members of the sub-clan are the owners (*toli*) of the sub-clan hamlet and its associated lands. The Trobriand sub-clan is a dispersed unit which seldom actually assembles all in one place; the sub-clan hamlet and its lands is on the other hand a permanent visible entity known to all. It is really an inversion of the facts to say that the continuing units in Trobriand social structure are the sub-clans and that the hamlets belong to the sub-clans. It is much closer to reality to say that the continuing units are the hamlets and that the sub-clan members belong to the hamlets by virtue of the emergence myths. How many kinds of sub-clan hamlet ought there to be in terms of Trobriand mythology?

The sub-clan emergence myths are mostly bald and perfunctory assertions of dogmatic fact, but they are supplemented by a much more elaborate story of the same type. 'Only one myth of first emergence is expanded into a long and dramatized story, and that is the myth of the first emergence of the four ancestors of the four main clans' (Malinowski 1935, 1: 343). In this myth the four totemic animals of the four clans emerge one after another from a single hole (Malinowski 1932: 419 f.). Malinowski maintains that the function of this myth is to assert the superior rank status of the Tabalu sub-clan of the Malasi clan, but his argument is weak. To me it seems plain that this 'clan' emergence myth can only be understood if considered along with the 'sub-clan' emergence myths. In that context what the myth 'says' is that while people in general are indissolubly associated with particular domains—sub-clan members with their sub-clan hamlets—there are four distinct kinds of such people.

My thesis is then that the four Trobriand clans are not really to be thought of as four unique and separate lines of descent—Trobrianders indeed seem to have little interest in pedigree. The four clans are an 'expression', a kind of model, of the fact that the Trobriand individual finds himself in a world which contains, so far as he is concerned, four kinds of localized hamlets with their associated sub-clans. From the young male Ego's point of view there are four categories of land-owners—*tama, kada, yawa, tabu*—and they have four categories of daughters—*luta, latu, yawa, tabu*. This explains why the importance of the four clans seems to be constantly emphasized by the Trobrianders themselves, even though the clans scarcely exist as corporate groups and may at times be difficult to identify at all.

CONCLUSION

In this paper I have sought to demonstrate the advantage of approaching the analysis of a kinship terminology without any preconceived assumption that the 'primary meaning' of this or that particular word must necessarily be defined by genealogy. My general standpoint is that kinship terms are category words by means of which the individual is taught to recognize the significant groupings in the social structure into which he is born. Until we as anthropologists fully understand the nature of that social structure we can hardly hope to understand what the various category words 'mean'. Indeed the meaning of particular terms varies according to the age status of the individual within the total system.

From Malinowski's writings we can safely infer that, in Trobriand social structure, descent group affiliation and residential grouping have an almost equal importance. We can further infer that the *urigubu* payment is the primary and fundamental expression of the various relationships which result from this structure. Assuming this to be the case, I have examined the kinship term categories against the structural background. The result is what seems to me a perfect 'fit'. Where the genealogical analysis of Malinowski leads to a maze of 'anomalies' and to Malinowski's desperate expedient of the doctrine of homonyms, the present analysis displays no exceptions and can in fact be memorized in a few minutes. This consistency convinces me that the pattern I have given comes very near to the Trobrianders own conception. Further confirmation is provided by the fit between the fourfold categories in the kinship system and the four clans. The supposed preference for patrilateral cross-cousin marriage has been demonstrated as an expression of the rules of exogamy which emerge from other elements in the structure. This much indeed Malinowski himself proclaimed, but where Malinowski argued that exogamy centred in the sub-clan and clan, I have suggested that it is based in the male Ego's dual residential status in the hamlets of his father and his mother's brother.

My further initial purpose was to demonstrate that there is an inherent consistency between all the various meanings of *tabu* which were listed at the beginning of this paper. This I claim to have done. In the context of kinship, *tabu* in all its senses is seen to refer to 'remote and potentially hostile relatives with whom Ego has no direct economic bonds but towards whom an attitude of "friendship" is expected'. It is a category of marginal relationship; it is filled with the 'dangers of the unknown' upon which Malinowski was prone to lay such stress. The category includes remote deceased ancestors and totemic spirits, and this links up the notion of 'sacred-forbidden' with that of 'distant-dangerous'.

Open hostility is not involved, *tabu* are related to one another only by intermediate links, there is no common economic interest which they are likely to fight about. But, for all that, *tabu* are dangerous people, people of power with whom you must be on good terms. It is significant that the only situations in which Malinowski mentions the *tabu* relationship as being ritually important are occasions when the *tabu* influence one another by magic (Malinowski 1932: 185 ff., 295 ff.). The magic in these cases happens to be beneficial, but a Trobriander would never forget that any magician may very easily become a sorcerer.

I hope then that I have disposed of the idea that the various meanings of *tabu* are accidental homonyms as unrelated as *pair* and *pear*.

Yet the puzzle remains. Why should Malinowski have been so keen to insist that the various meanings of the word are wholly unrelated. Why, when he himself laid such stress on the taboo between a man and his sister, should he repudiate the logic by which a boy regards his father's sister as *tabu*?

The answer seems to be that it was because he took over uncritically from his predecessors the bland assumption that the key to the understanding of any system of kinship terminology must always be sought in rules of preferred marriage.

This belief had been dogma for Rivers, and Malinowski regarded Rivers' anthropology as the very quintessence of everything that is wrong-headed and misdirected. Yet Malinowski's pronouncements regarding the term *tabu* seem to derive from the fact that Trobrianders told him that they ought to marry their *tabu*. How could it possibly be that the term which thus described the 'lawful woman' should also mean 'forbidden, dangerous, sacred'? The only possible explanation for Malinowski was that we are here dealing with two or more entirely different words. What he failed to notice was that when a man does marry a *tabu* relative either close or remote, she and her immediate kinsmen forthwith cease to be *tabu*, and come into the much more closely bonded categories of *lubou* and *yawa*. In other words, marriage is a device whereby the dangers of *tabu* are for the time being exorcized.

NOTES

[1] Malinowski (1932: 52) translates *toboma* as 'tabooed man' from the general root *boma* ('sacred', 'taboo'). This fits well with the explanation of *tabu* given below.

[2] Source Powell. In strict formality father's mother's mother's brothers are *tama*, mother's mother's brothers are *kada*. The informal use of *tabu* here seems to fit with the use of *toboma* for certain respected old men; cf. p.126.

[3] It is possible that some members of either of these two hamlets might be members of Ego's own sub-clan. In that case he would use *kada, ina, tuwa, bwada, luta* as appropriate in place of *tabu*.

[4] Mr Powell has here corrected Malinowski. The term *ivata* which appears in Malinowski's lists is not used by males and I shall not discuss it. In Malinowski, *yawa* has the restricted meaning of parent-in-law.

[5] The Kwoynama sub-clan itself possibly has a similar arrangement with their political inferiors of the Malasi clan in the village of Yalumugwa. Malinowski (1935: 389) shows the Kwoynama village headman Yovisi marrying off his sister Aykare'i to his own wife's brother who is a member of the inferior Malasi sub-clan in the same village as Yovisi himself.

Cf. also Seligman (1910: 718) where it is noted that *for chiefs only* the father, the children and the sisters' husbands fall into one ritual category; this would be a logical consequence of bilateral cross-cousin marriage.

REFERENCES CITED

Evans-Pritchard, E. E. 1951, *Kinship and Marriage among the Nuer*, Oxford.
Firth, R. (Editor) 1956, *Man and Culture*, London.
Fortes, M. 1949 (*a*), 'Time and Social Structure: An Ashanti Case Study' in Fortes, M. (ed.) *Social Structure*, Oxford.
—— 1949 (*b*), *The Web of Kinship among the Tallensi*, London.
—— 1953, 'The structure of unilineal descent Groups', *American Anthropologist*, 55.
Gilbert, W. H. 1937, 'Eastern Chérokee Social Organization' in Eggan, F. (ed.) *Social Anthropology of North American Tribes*, Chicago.
Homans, G. C. and Schneider, D. M. 1955, *Marriage Authority and Final Causes*, Glencoe, Illinois.
Leach, E. R. 1945, 'Jinghpaw Kinship Terminology', *J.R.A.I.* LXXV.
Malinowski, B. 1922, *Argonauts of the Western Pacific*, London.
—— 1932, *The Sexual Life of Savages* (3rd ed.), London.
—— 1935, *Coral Gardens and their Magic*, 2 vols. London.
Radcliffe-Brown, A. R. 1933, *The Andaman Islanders* (2nd ed.), London.
—— 1952, *Structure and Function in Primitive Society*, London.
Seligman, C. G. 1910, *The Melanesians of British New Guinea*, Cambridge.
Tax, Sol. 1937, 'Some Problems of Social Organization' in Eggan, F. (ed.) *Social Anthropology of North American Tribes*, Chicago.
Tylor, E. B. 1888, 'On a Method of Investigating the Development of Institutions: Applied to Laws of Marriage and Descent', *J.R.A.I.* LVIII.
White, L. A. 1948, 'The Definition and Prohibition of Incest', *American Anthropologist*, 50.